First Settlers

in

Georgia

Volume 2

Abstracts of English Crown Grants
in
St. George Parish, 1755–1775

Burke, Glascock, Jefferson, Jenkins
and Screven Counties

Pat Bryant

Surveyor General Department
State of Georgia

Heritage Books
2024

HERITAGE BOOKS
AN IMPRINT OF HERITAGE BOOKS, INC.

Books, CDs, and more—Worldwide

For our listing of thousands of titles see our website
at
www.HeritageBooks.com

A Facsimile Reprint
Published 2024 by
HERITAGE BOOKS, INC.
Publishing Division
5810 Ruatan Street
Berwyn Heights, MD 20740

Originally Printed 1974
by the State Printing Office
Atlanta, Georgia

Reprinted by Special Permission of
Georgia State Archives
1998

International Standard Book Number
Paperbound: 978-0-7884-2662-9

Introduction

The Royal Charter of June, 1732, given by King George II to
the Trustees for Establishing the Colony of Georgia in America,
defined the boundaries of the new colony as lying between the
Savannah and Altamaha Rivers, extending as far north as those
rivers flowed and thence from their sources in a straight line
to the South Seas.

The land in question was in possession of the Creek and Cherokee
Nations, and when James Edward Oglethorpe, one of the Trustees
and the leader of the colony, landed at Yamacraw Bluff on the
Savannah River on February 12, 1733, he was well aware that
some agreement with the Indians was necessary. His first treaty
with the Creeks in 1733 assured him of a small area along the
Savannah River, running north along it to a point opposite
today's Rincon, passing through that town and today's Eden in
a diagonal line to the Ogeechee, thence south and a little
west in a straight line to the Altamaha River, or, as it has
been described elsewhere, "the area between the Savannah and
the Altamaha as high as the tides flowed." This was the small
part of the original charter grant in which the colonists settled and here they laid out the City of Savannah.

The 1733 Treaty with the Creeks reserved two parcels of land
for themselves. One was an area from Pipemaker's Bluff to
Palachucolas Creek and the other was the Islands of Ossabaw,
Sapelo, and St. Catherine. It was not until 1757 at a congress
held as Savannah that a treaty between the English and the
Creeks gave to Georgia the three great Sea Islands and the
small tract of land in reserve near Savannah. By this time,
too, the colonists had settled considerably beyond the limits
of the first treaty and came to look upon all this land as
their own. Oglethorpe had early fortified St. Simons Island
knowing well that it was outside of the treaty boundary as
well as the charter limits. The next year in 1758, without
treaty or permissions from the Indians, an Act of the Assembly
created seven parishes, i.e., St. Paul, St. George, St. Matthew, Chrish Church, St. Philip, St. John and St. Andrew.
By Royal Proclamation in 1763, the English Crown extended
Georgia's southern boundary to the St. Marys River, and by
Act of Assembly again, the four new parishes of St. David,
St. Patrick, St. Thomas and St. Mary were created from that
extension in 1765.

The Creeks were uneasy about these expansions and in order to
quiet them and to redefine the western boundary, a new treaty

was made in 1763 at Augusta. The limits of the settlers went
as far as the Little River to the north, down the Ogeechee
to the southwest corner of the present boundary line of Bul-
loch County, southward crossing the upper reaches of the
Canoochee River and ended at the St. Marys.

The last of the Royal Provincial treaties was in 1773 and this
included what was called the Ceded Lands, a rich area acquired
from the Creeks and Cherokees north of the Little River to the
Broad and west almost to the Oconee River. Settlement in this
area was barely begun when the first fires of the Revolution
were seen in the Province and until that war was over, Georgia
remained a relatively narrow strip along the Savannah to the
Ogeechee River.

Under the Trustees, from 1732 until the charter was resigned
to the Crown in 1752, all allottments or leases of land made
to the settlers were in Tail Male. Unlike fee simple grants,
the leases could not be mortgaged, sold or otherwise disposed
with. Some confusion exists about these allottments and
leases, since some of the written records refer to them as
grants, when, strictly speaking, that term is not correct. In
1752, after the relinquishment of the charter, Georgia became
a Royal Province and under the English Crown and its Royal
Governors, fee simple grants were made to the land which gave
a clear title to the grantees. These Royal Grants, in the
Georgia Surveyor General Department of the Office of the
Secretary of State, begin in 1755. The three year gap between
1752 and 1755 is variously explained by historians, but in any
case, the latter year is the first date for the grants. There
are some 5000 of these recorded.

The department has now abstracted, very carefully and accurately,
all of the Royal Provincial Grants. Using cards, citations to
survey date, grant date, acres, name of grantee, page and book
of record are shown, and a verbatim extraction of the description
of the property granted. The legal verbiage of "Appurtenances
and hereditaments" has been omitted. All else is shown in the
abstract.

During the Revolution, according to one of the state's early
Surveyors General, many of the plats of survey for the Royal
Grants were destroyed. In abstracting the grants, it was
found that only one grant in four had the plat of survey. Also,
some plats existed for which there was no grant issued, although
there were not many of these. In the text, where the reader

Introduction

finds no citation for a survey, there is none, and, conversely, where no grant is shown, there is none extant.

It is hoped that this effort will give important data to state officials first, and then to geographers, historians and the general public.

Transition from Districts and Towns into
Parishes in 1758 and 1765 to Counties in 1777

1732 - 1758 Districts & Towns	1758 - 1765 Parishes	1765 - 1777 Parishes	1777 Counties
District of Augusta	St. Paul	St. Paul	Richmond
District of Halifax	St. George	St. George	Burke
District of Abercorn	St. Matthew	St. Matthew	Effingham
District of Goshen	St. Matthew	St. Matthew	Effingham
District of Ebenezer	St. Matthew	St. Matthew	Effingham
District of Ogechee (above Canoochee River)	St. Philip	St. Philip	Effingham
District of Ogechee (below Canoochee River)	St. Philip	St. Philip	Chatham
Town of Hardwick	St. Philip	St. Philip	Chatham
Town of Savannah	Christ Church	Christ Church	Chatham
District of Savannah	Christ Church	Christ Church	Chatham
Sea Islands north of Great Ogechee River	Christ Church	Christ Church	Chatham
Town of Sunbury	St. John	St. John	Liberty
District of Midway	St. John	St. John	Liberty
District of Newport	St. John	St. John	Liberty
St. Catherines Island	St. John	St. John	Liberty
Bermuda Island	St. John	St. John	Liberty
Town of Darien	St. Andrew	St. Andrew	Liberty
District of Darien	St. Andrew	St. Andrew	Liberty
Sapelo Island	St. Andrew	St. Andrew	Liberty
Eastwood Island	St. Andrew	St. Andrew	Liberty
Sea Islands between Great Ogechee & Altamaha Rivers	St. Andrew	St. Andrew	Liberty
Town of Frederica	St. James	St. James	Liberty
District of Frederica	St. James	St. James	Liberty
Great St. Simons Island	St. James	St. James	Liberty
Little St. Simons Island	St. James	St. James	Liberty
Sea Islands south of Altamaha River	St. James	St. James	Liberty
Between Altamaha & Turtle River		St. David	Glynn
Between Turtle and Little Satilla Rivers		St. Patrick	Glynn
Between Little Satilla & Great Satilla Rivers		St. Thomas	Camden
Between Great Satilla & St. Marys River		St. Mary	Camden

Horatio Marbury & William H. Crawford. Digest of the Laws of Georgia (Savannah 1802) P. 150-153.

State of Georgia. 1777 Constitution, Section 242.

Adams, William
300 acres in St. George Parish

Granted on January 1, 1765   Grant Book E, page 88

300 acres bounded on the northeast and northwest by Lewis
Boynum, James Carter, vacant land and McIntosh's Swamp.

****

Adams, William
200 acres in St. George Parish

Granted on January 1, 1765   Grant Book E, page 89

200 acres bounded on the southeast by Lewis Bynon, on the
northeast by James Carter and on all other sides by vacant
land.

****

Alday, Josiah
150 acres in St. George Parish

Granted on December 4, 1770   Grant Book I, page 212

150 acres bounded on the southeast by John Thomas and on all
other sides by vacant land.

****

Alexander, David
550 acres in St. George Parish

Granted on December 6, 1774   Grant Book M, page 771

Town Lot 18 in Queensborough and 550 acres bounded on the
southwest by Robert Brieson and vacant land and on the
northeast by Samuel Gibson.

****

Alexander, Hugh
100 acres in St. George Parish

Granted on September 6, 1774   Grant Book M, page 279

100 acres in Queensborough Township bounded on the southeast
by John and Thomas Gibson.

****

Alexander, Samuel
48 acres in St. George Parish

Granted on June 5, 1764   Grant Book E, page 13

48 acres bounded on the south by James Nelson and on all
other sides by the Savannah River.

****

Alexander, Samuel
100 acres in St. George Parish

Granted on June 5, 1764   Grant Book E, page 14

100 acres bounded on the east by the Savannah River, on the
north by James Nelson, on the west by Benjamin Horn and on
the south by vacant land.

****

Alexander, William
100 acres in St. George Parish

Granted on September 6, 1774   Grant Book M, page 280

100 acres in Queensborough Township and bounded on the
southeast by Dry Creek and on all other sides by vacant land.

****

Alger, Preserved
250 acres in St. George Parish

Granted on November 1, 1768   Grant Book G, page 207

250 acres bounded on the west by Robert Hudson, on the southeast by Briar Creek and on every other side by vacant land.

****

Allan, John
150 acres in St. George Parish

Granted on November 5, 1771   Grant Book I, page 446

150 acres bounded on the west by Lucy Clark, other sides vacant.

****

Anderson, Augustus H.
150 acres in St. George Parish

Original survey date unknown
Resurveyed on February 6, 1838   Plat Book M, page 129
Granted on March 3, 1767   Grant Book F, page 105

150 acres bounded on the south by the Great Ogechee River,
southeast by the said Daniel Douglass. Resurveyed for
Augustus H. Anderson.

****

Anderson, David
100 acres in St. George Parish

Granted on September 6, 1774   Grant Book M, page 278

100 acres bounded on the north and west by land formerly
owned by James Anderson, deceased, and south by James Gordon.

****

Anderson, Elizabeth
150 acres in St. George Parish

Granted on October 29, 1765   Grant Book E, page 323

150 acres bounded on the northeast by Henry Overstreet and
on the north by the said Elizabeth Anderson.

****

Anderson, Elizabeth
150 acres in St. George Parish

Granted on August 5, 1766   Grant Book E, page 324

150 acres bounded on the northeast by Henry Overstreet and
south by the said Elizabeth Anderson.

****

Anderson, James
500 acres in St. George Parish

Surveyed on September 19, 1761   Plat Book C, page 2
Granted on May 21, 1762   Grant Book D, page 100

500 acres bounded on the west by William Rains and on all other sides by vacant land. The original warrant states that "500 acres on Bowers Branch joining the east line of the lands granted William Raines in Hallifax District.

****

Anderson, James
400 acres in St. George Parish

Granted on July 3, 1764   Grant Book E, apge 24

400 acres located on Rocky Creek, bounded by the said James Anderson on the east and on all other sides by vacant land.

****

Anderson, James
150 acres in St. George Parish

Granted on February 3, 1767   Grant Book F, page 51

150 acres bounded on the south by Joseph Dunlap, on the north by the said James Anderson and on all other sides vacant.

****

Anderson, John
150 acres in St. George Parish

Surveyed on April 14, 1767   Plat Book C, page 1
Granted on August 2, 1768   Grant Book G, page 146

150 acres bounded on the southwest by the said John Anderson. This tract was part of 300 acres heretofore ordered to and surveyed for John Sharp.

****

Anderson, John
150 acres in St. George Parish

Surveyed on April 14, 1767   Plat Book M, page 6
Granted on August 2, 1768   Grant Book G, page 147

150 acres bounded on the northeast by said John Anderson. This tract was part of 300 acres heretofore ordered to and surveyed for John Sharp.

****

Anderson, John
100 acres in St. George Parish

Granted on January 7, 1772   Grant Book I, page 486

100 acres bounded on all sides by vacant land.

                              ****

Anderson, John
100 acres in St. George Parish

Granted on July 3, 1770   Grant Book M, page 2

100 acres in Queensborough bounded on the northwest by Patrick
McGie and northeast by ------Hambleton.

                              ****

Armstrong, Matthew
100 acres in St. George Parish

Granted on November 1, 1774   Grant Book M, page 617

100 acres bounded on the northeast by David Emanuel and on
all other sides by vacant land.

                              ****

Arthur, Francis
100 acres in St. George Parish

Granted on November 1, 1774   Grant Book M, page 616

100 acres bounded on all sides by vacant land.

                              ****

Asbell, John
50 acres in St. George Parish

Granted on July 5, 1763   Grant Book D, page 312

50 acres bounded on all sides by vacant land.

                              ****

Asberry, Landman
150 acres in St. George Parish

Granted on May 4, 1773   Grant Book I, page 965

150 acres bounded on the northeast by land of William Adams and on all other sides by vacant land.

****

Atkinson, Joseph
126 acres in St. George Parish

Granted on June 6, 1769   Grant Book G, page 324

126 acres being the surplus measure of a tract of land heretofore granted to his father, Joshua Atkinson, deceased, and said to contain but 200 acres, the whole tract containing together 376 acres. 126 acres bounded on the southeast and northwest by vacant land and on all other sides by John Thomas, Jr.

****

Attaway, Harley
150 acres in St. George Parish

Original survey date unknown   Plat Book M, page 111
Granted on September 1, 1767   Grant Book F, page 349

150 acres bounded on the northwest by John Howell, the southwest by John Rae, the southeast by Andrew Lambert. Resurveyed for William Green and Harley Attaway on August 18, 1824 and found to contain 175 acres. Surveyed on granted to David Howell originally. See DAVID HOWELL.

****

Audley, Gerrard
350 acres in St. George Parish

Granted on April 7, 1772   Grant Book I, page 542

350 acres bounded on the south by William Jordan, north by James Hall and on all other sides by vacant land.

****

Austin, Davis
100 acres in St. George Parish

Granted on July 5, 1768   Grant Book G, page 131

100 acres bounded on the north by Elizabeth Burney, southwest by Paul Austin, northeast by Drury Austin and on all other sides by vacant land.

****

Austin, Drury
100 acres in St. George Parish

Granted on July 5, 1768   Grant Book G, page 132

loo acres bounded on the northwest by Elizabeth Burney and on the southwest by David Austin.

****

Austin, Paul
100 acres in St. George Parish

Granted on July 5, 1768   Grant Book G, page 133

100 acres bounded on the northeast by Davis Austin and on all other sides by vacant land.

****

Averitt, Jehu
150 acres in St. George Parish

Granted on April 6, 1770   Grant Book I, page 932

150 acres bounded on the west by John Lott, Jr., on the southeast by James Fletcher and on all other sides by vacant land.

****

Backam, James
400 acres in St. George Parish

Granted on April 5, 1768   Grant Book G, page 65

400 acres bounded on the northeast by William Johnston and on all other sides by vacant land.

****

Baggs, John
100 acres in St. George Parish

Granted on January 3, 1775   Grant Book M, page 855

100 acres in Queensborough bounded on the north by John Brown and vacant land, west by Lamberts Creek, east by Thomas Irvin and south by George Spiers.

****

Bags, Alexander
100 acres in St. George Parish

Granted on July 3, 1770   Grant Book I, page 89

Lot 68 in the Town of Queensborough and 100 acres in the Township bounded on the east by Lamberts Creek.

****

Bailey, Joseph
150 acres in St. George Parish

Granted on December 4, 1770   Grant Book I, page 213

150 acres in Queensborough Towsnhip bounded on all sides by vacant land.

****

Baillie, George
400 acres in St. George Parish

Granted on November 1, 1774   Grant Book M, page 628

400 acres bounded on all sides by vacant land.

****

Baillie, George
500 acres in St. George Parish

Granted on December 6, 1774   Grant Book M, page 838

500 acres bounded on the southeast by Thomas Samuel and southwest by the Great Ogechee River.

****

Baillie, George and Houstoun, John
1000 acres in St. George Parish

Granted on August 2, 1774   Grant Book M, page 208

1000 acres bounded on the southeast by Thomas Lewis and southwest by Walker and Thomas Yarborough.

****

Baker, Henry
400 acres in St. George Parish

Granted on April 7, 1767   Grant Book F, page 154

400 acres situate about 3 miles above the mouth of Bark Camp at a branch called the Big Branch.

****

Baker, Henry
150 acres in St. George Parish

Granted on November 3, 1767   Grant Book F, page 399

150 acres bounded on the southwest by the Ogechee River and on the east and north by the said Henry Baker.

****

Balsh, Thomas
100 acres in St. George Parish

Granted on October 29, 1765   Grant Book E, page 303

100 acres located on Rosemary Branch and bounded on all sides by vacant land.

****

Barron, Rheuben
150 acres in St. George Parish

Granted on August 2, 1774   Grant Book M, page 155

150 acres bounded on all sides by vacant land.

****

Barron, Richard
200 acres in St. George Parish

Granted on August 2, 1774   Grant Book M, page 161

200 acres bounded on all sides by vacant land.

****

Barron, Richard
150 acres in St. George Parish

Granted on August 2, 1774   Grant Book M, page 162

150 acres bounded on the northwest by Richard Barron and on
the northeast by James Carter.

****

Barry, George
500 acres in St. George Parish

Granted on June 7, 1774   Grant Book I, page 1081

500 acres bounded on the northeast by Daniel O'Sheal and
Moses Fusil and southwest by ----Young and Hardy Boykin.

****

Bartholomew, John
100 acres in St. George Parish

Granted on July 3, 1770   Grant Book I, page 90

100 acres bounded on the east by Ruby Branch, partly on the
north by Matthew Sykes and part vacant land, on the south
by James Thompson and west by vacant land, being in the
Township of Queensborough, and also lot 69 in the Town
of Queensborough.

****

Bass, Matthew
200 acres in St. George Parish

Granted on January 3, 1775   Grant Book M, page 853

200 acres bounded on the northeast and on the southeast by
-----Douglass and on the northwest by Roundtree.

****

Baulch, Thomas
100 acres in St. George Parish

Granted on August 2, 1774   Grant Book M, page 163

100 acres bounded on the southeast by William Peters and on all other sides by vacant land.

****

Beal, Jacob
200 acres in St. George Parish

Granted on November 1, 1774   Grant Book M, page 631

200 acres bounded on all sides by vacant land.

****

Beatty, James
250 acres in St. George Parish

Granted on September 6, 1774   Grant Book M, page 281

250 acres in Queensborough bounded on all sides by vacant land.

****

Beatty, Joseph
500 acres in St. George Parish

Granted on June 7, 1774   Grant Book I, page 1065

500 acres in the Township of Queensborough bounded on the west by William Skelly and John Martin, east by William Skelly, Jr. and Lambert Creek, south by Robert Gervin and north by Alex Beggs; and also lot 36 in Queensborough Township.

****

Beatty, Thomas
150 acres in St. George Parish

Granted on July 3, 1770   Grant Book I, page 88

150 acres bounded on the north by James Thompson, partly on the south by David Graves and partly by vacant land, and

east by Ruby Branch and west by vacant land; and also lot 16 in the Town of Queensborough.

****

Beckham, Simon
200 acres in St. George Parish

Granted on September 6, 1768   Grant Book G, page 170

200 acres bounded on the west by James Stiggams and on all other sides by vacant land.

****

Bell, Christian
300 acres in St. George Parish

Granted on December 3, 1771   Grant Book I, page 468

300 acres bounded on all sides by vacant land.

****

Bell, Thomas
200 acres in St. George Parish

Surveyed on August 10, 1759   Plat Book C, page 31

200 acres bounded on the north by the Savannah River and on the west by Thomas Cockran. The original warrant states, "200 acres on Savannah River about four miles above Stony Bluff in the District of Halifax joining lands of William Cockran.

****

Bennett, William
300 acres in St. George Parish

Granted on January 7, 1772   Grant Book I, page 488

300 acres bounded on the southwest by Ann Terrigan and on all other sides by vacant land.

****

Bennett, William
250 acres in St. George Parish

Original survey date unknown   Plat Book M, page 130
Granted on October 2, 1770   Grant Book I, page 170

250 acres resurveyed for William Bennett and found to
contain 261½ acres.

****

Berryhill, Alexander
250 acres in St. George Parish

Granted on May 4, 1773   Grant Book I, page 969

250 acres bounded on the northeast by Patrick Butler, northwest by Samuel Clark and west by George Galphin and Quintin
Pooler.

****

Berryhill, Andrew
100 acres in St. George Parish

Granted on February 7, 1769   Grant Book G, page 263

100 acres bound on all sides by vacant land.

****

Berryhill, Andrew
100 acres in St. George Parish

Granted on July 5, 1774   Grant Book M, page 7

100 acres bounded on the east by Absalom Wells and on all
other sides by vacant land.

****

Bevill, Robert
550 acres in St. George Parish

Surveyed on December 31, 1760   Plat Book C, page 30
Granted on May 21, 1762   Grant Book D, page 86

550 acres bounded on the east by the Savannah River. The
original warrant states, "550 acres about four miles above
Briar Creek and three quarters of a mile above land granted
John Conyers.

****

Beville, Sarah, widow
300 acres in St. George Parish

Granted on January 5, 1768   Grant Book G, page 1

300 acres bounded on the east by Briar Creek and on all other sides by vacant land.

****

Bickham, James
100 acres in St. George Parish

Granted on September 6, 1774   Grant Book M, page 283

100 acres bounded on all sides by vacant land.

****

Bird, Sylvanus
100 acres in St. George Parish

Granted on March 3, 1767   Grant Book F, page 98

100 acres bounded on the northwest by Israel Bird and south-east by John Redwike.

****

Blair, James
100 acres in St. George Parish

Granted on July 3, 1770   Grant Book I, page 92

100 acres in the Township of Queensborough and also lot 47 in the Town of Queensborough.

****

Blanchard, Robert
150 acres in St. George Parish

Granted on September 6, 1774   Grant Book M, page 284

150 acres bounded on all sides by vacant land.

****

Bland, William
200 acres in St. George Parish

Granted on September 3, 1765   Grant Book E, page 224

200 acres bounded on all sides by vacant land.

****

Bland, William
100 acres in St. George Parish

Granted on March 3, 1767   Grant Book F, page 96

100 acres bounded on the north by the Savannah River and on the southeast by James Gray.

****

Bledsoe, John
100 acres in St. George Parish

Granted on June 2, 1772   Grant Book I, page 646

100 acres bounded on all sides by vacant land.

****

Blyth, Peter
300 acres in St. George Parish

Granted on July 7, 1761   Grant Book C, page 152

300 acres bounded on the north by Robert Bevil, northeast by the Savannah River and southeast by John Conyers.

****

Blyth, Peter and Ring, Christopher
400 acres in St. George Parish

Granted on October 2, 1764   Grant Book E, page 49

400 acres on Rocky Creek, originally surveyed for Charles Gee, but granted to Blyth and Ring as creditors of Gee.

****

Boit, William
250 acres in St. George Parish

Granted on June 5, 1770   Grant Book I, page 17

250 acres bounded on the east by Robert Prior and on the northwest by Robert Bowling.

****

Bolton, John
71 acres in St. George Parish

Granted on January 3, 1775   Grant Book M, page 848

71 acres bounded on the north by the Savannah River, on the northwest by Humphrey and southeast by Sleather.

****

Boosman, James
100 acres in St. George Parish

Granted on August 2, 1774   Grant Book M, page 156

100 acres bounded on the south by the Great Ogechee River and on all other sides by vacant land.

****

Borneman, Benjamin William
500 acres in St. George Parish

Granted on April 13, 1761   Grant Book C, page 310

500 acres bounded on the north by Catherine Magdalen Greiner, wife of John Gasper Greiner, on the east by the Savannah River and on the south by the glebe land.

****

Bowey, James
150 acres in St. George Parish

Granted on May 3, 1768   Grant Book G, page 93

150 acres bounded on the east by John Burney and on all other sides by vacant land.

****

Bowie, James
200 acres in St. George Parish

Granted on June 5, 1770   Grant Book I, page 15

200 acres bounded partly on the northwest and southeast by William Case and land vacant, on the southeast by Dancie Douglas, and on the northeast by Briar Creek.

****

Bowling, Robert
200 acres in St. George Parish

Granted on June 5, 1770   Grant Book I, page 18

200 acres bounded 200 acres bounded on all sides by vacant land.

****

Bowling, Robert
100 acres in St. George Parish

Granted on September 6, 1774   Grant Book M, page 285

100 acres bounded on all sides by vacant land.

****

Bowman, John
1600 acres in St. George Parish

Surveyed on April 18, 1770   Plat Book M, page 27
Granted October 2, 1770   Grant Book I, page 167

1600 acres bounded on the southwest by Richard Womack, Jesse Womack and John Emannce, partly on the southeast by James Lambeth and Anthony Stokes and land vacant, northwest by Isaac Eaton and on all other sides by vacant land.

****

Bowman, John
400 acres in St. George Parish

Granted on February 7, 1775   Grant Book M, page 979

400 acres bounded on the southeast by John Rogers and on all other sides by vacant land.

****

Boyd, Joseph
100 acres in St. George Parish

Granted on March 2, 1773   Grant Book I, page 911

100 acres in Queensborough Township, bounded on the west
by Samuel Gibson, on the north by Adam Morrison and on
all other sides by vacant land.

****

Boykin, Edward
200 acres in St. George Parish

Granted on April 7, 1767   Grant Book F, page 217

200 acres bounded on the south by Bryar Creek, west partly
by John Brantly and land vacant, east partly by David Green
and land vacant and north by vacant land.

****

Boykin, Solomon
200 acres in St. George Parish

Granted on May 5, 1767   Grant Book F, page 218

200 acres bounded on the west by John Wills and on all other
sides by vacant land.

****

Boykin, Solomon
300 acres in St. George Parish

Granted on April 5, 1768   Grant Book G, page 67

300 acres bounded on all sides by vacant land.

****

Bracy, Randal
300 acres in St. George Parish

Granted November 1, 1768   Grant Book G, page 210

300 acres bounded on the west by part of Jethro Roundtree's
land and on all other sides by vacant land.

****

Bradley, John
350 acres in St. George Parish

Granted on December 3, 1760   Grant Book C, page 13

350 acres bounded on the northeast by the Savannah River, south by Robert Bevil and north by Nathaniel Miller.

****

Bradley, John
400 acres in St. George Parish

Granted on January 2, 1770   Grant Book G, page 491

400 acres bounded on the southwest by Nickolas Cavenah and on all other sides by vacant land.

****

Brady, Patrick
200 acres in St. George Parish

Granted on May 5, 1770   Grant Book I, page 16

200 acres bounded on the northwest by William Moxley and land vacant, southeast partly by land of the said Patrick Brady and on all other sides by vacant land.

****

Brady, Patrick
250 acres in St. George Parish

Original date of survey unknown
Resurveyed on June 1, 1838   Plat Book M, page 130
Granted on October 2, 1770   Grant Book I, page 170

250 acres resurveyed for William Bennett and found to contain 261½ acres.

****

Brantley, James
200 acres in St. George Parish

Granted on September 1, 1767   Grant Book F, page 338

200 acres bounded on all sides by vacant land.

****

Brantley, John
100 acres in St. George Parish

Granted on April 7, 1767   Grant Book F, page 156

100 acres bounded on all sides by vacant land.

****

Brantley, Thomas
150 acres in St. George Parish

Granted on June 2, 1767   Grant Book F, page 265

150 acres bounded on all sides by vacant land.

****

Brasher, Jesse
100 acres in St. George Parish

Granted on May 2, 1769   Grant Book G, page 311

100 acres bounded on the south by the said Jesse Brasher on
Horse Creek and bounded on all other sides by vacant land.

****

Braswell, Kendred
100 acres in St. George Parish

Granted on January 5, 1768   Grant Book G, page 2

100 acres bounded on all sides by vacant land.

****

Braswell, Robert
100 acres in St. George Parish

Granted on October 6, 1767   Grant Book F, page 376

100 acres bounded on all sides by vacant land.

****

Brazeal, Elijah
150 acres in St. George Parish

Granted on March 5, 1771   Grant Book I, page 262

150 acres bounded on the northeast by land of the said grantee and on the southeast by John Goode.

****

Breazeal, Elijah
300 acres in St. George Parish

Granted on April 4, 1769   Grant Book G, page 296

300 acres bounded on the south by Daniel Lot and on all other sides by vacant land.

****

Breazeal, Elijah
150 acres in St. George Parish

Granted on October 4, 1774   Grant Book M, page 422

150 acres bounded on the southeast by Henry Baker, northwest by Peter Winn and vacant land, northeast by vacant land and south and west by the Great Ogechee River.

****

Briggs, James
250 acres in St. George Parish

Granted on May 3, 1768   Grant Book G, page 92

250 acres bounded on all sides by vacant land.

****

Brown, James
100 acres in St. George Parish

Granted on November 5, 1771   Grant Book I, page 448

100 acres bounded partly on the northeast and partly on the southeast by John Harvey and on all other sides by vacant land.

****

Brown, James
100 acres in St. George Parish

Granted on February 7, 1775   Grant Book M, page 977

100 acres bounded on the southwest by the said James Brown and on all other sides by vacant land.

****

Brown, John
200 acres in St. George Parish

Granted on July 3, 1770   Grant Book I, page 91

Lot 46 in the Township of Queensborough and also 200 acres in the said township bounded on the northwest by Lamberts Creek.

****

Brown, Richard
150 acres in St. George Parish

Granted on October 1, 1771   Grant Book I, page 426

150 acres bounded on the north by Thomas Red and on all other sides by vacant land.

****

Brown, William
200 acres in St. George Parish

Granted on April 7, 1767   Grant Book F, page 221

200 acres bounded on the northwest by Isaac Copeland and on all other sides by vacant land.

****

Brown, William
100 acres in St. George Parish

Surveyed on June 4, 1772   Plat Book C, page 23

Warrant states that, "200 acres between Brier Creek and McBeans Swamp bounded on the southwest by Richard Brown.

****

Brunell, Anthony
200 acres in St. George Parish

Granted on September 3, 1765   Grant Book E, page 223

200 acres bounded on all sides by vacant land.

****

Brunson, John
300 acres in St. George Parish

Granted on September 5, 1760   Grant Book C, page 1

300 acres bounded on the southeast by John McNish and northwest by John Conyers.

****

Brunson, John
200 acres in St. George Parish

Granted on May 3, 1768   Grant Book G, page 94

200 acres bounded on the southwest by Briar Creek, east by
Benjamin Moodie and on all other sides by vacant land.

****

Bryson, Robert
250 acres in St. George Parish

Granted on July 5, 1774   Grant Book M, page 8

250 acres in Queensborough Township bounded on the south
corner by ----Crosley and on all other sides by vacant land.

****

Burgess, Samuel
100 acres in St. George Parish

Granted on December 6, 1774   Grant Book M, page 774

100 acres bounded on all sides by vacant land.

****

Burnet, Charles
2000 acres in either St. George or St. Paul Parish

Original survey date unknown
Resurveyed on July 19, 1803   Plat Book M, page 55
Granted on May 2, 1769   Grant Book G, page 309

2000 acres bounded on the southwest by Sir James Wright and James Habersham, on the northwest by Thomas Netherclift and vacant land. By checking the plat of survey of Thomas Netherclift above, of record at page 39 in Plat Book M one notes that his land was in St. George Parish. The resurvey shows this tract to be in Jefferson County, Georgia. The resurvey was made for General James Jackson and states, "a tract of land originally granted to Charles Burnett for 2000 acres but found on resurvey to contain 2014 acres which is now in possession of General James Jackson. Jefferson County was made up of parts of both St. George and St. Paul Parish or Burke and Richmond Counties.

****

Burney, Elizabeth
300 acres in St. George Parish

Granted on March 3, 1767   Grant Book F, page 94

300 acres on the north side of Buckhead Creek and bounded on the west by land of James Howell and on the south by Buckhead Creek. Granted to Elizabeth Burney during the term of her natural life and from and after her decease, to her son, Simon Burney.

****

Burney, Elizabeth
100 acres in St. George Parish

Granted on January 5, 1768   Grant Book G, page 3

100 acres bounded on the southeast by land laid out for a township and on all other sides by vacant land.

****

Burney, John
150 acres in St. George Parish

Granted on August 2, 1768   Grant Book G, page 150

150 acres bounded on the west by James Bowie and on all other sides by vacant land.

****

Burney, Simon
300 acres in St. George Parish

Granted on March 3, 1767   Grant Book F, page 94

300 acres on the north side of Buckhead Creek and bounded on the west by land ordered James Howel and on the south by Buckhead Creek. Granted to Elizabeth Burney during the term of her natural life and from and after her decease to Simon Burney, son of Elizabeth Burney.

****

Burney, William
150 acres in St. George Parish

Granted on August 4, 1767   Grant Book F, page 310

150 acres bounded on all sides by vacant land.

****

Burney, William
150 acres in St. George Parish

Granted on April 5, 1768   Grant Book G, page 68

150 acres bounded on all sides by vacant land.

****

Burnsides, John
200 acres in St. George Parish

Granted on May 1, 1764   Grant Book E, page 11

200 acres bounded on the northeast by William Standley, southeast by Thomas Caudrey and southwest by William Mainer and vacant land.

****

Burrington, Thomas
300 acres in St. George Parish

Granted on July 2, 1765   Grant Book E, page 188

300 acres bounded on the south by the Great Ogechee River and on the west by Daniel O'Cain and the said Thomas Burrington.

****

Burrington, Thomas
200 acres in St. George Parish

Granted on July 2, 1765   Grant Book E, page 189

200 acres bounded on the south by the Great Ogechee River and
on the north by Daniel O'Cain and the said Thomas Burrington.

****

Burton, Joseph
375 acres in St. George Parish

Surveyed on December 11, 1764   Plat Book C, page 23

375 acres located on Lamberts Creek and bounded on all other
sides by vacant land.

****

Bynon, Lewis
100 acres in St. George Parish

Granted on September 5, 1758   Grant Book B, page 44

100 acres bounded on the northeast and northwest by branches
of Bryer Creek and on all other sides by vacant land.

****

Cade, Bud
100 acres in St. George Parish

Granted on November 1, 1774   Grant Book M, page 635

100 acres bounded on the east and northwest by James Murphy
and on all other sides by vacant land.

****

Cade, John
100 acres in St. George Parish

Granted on December 6, 1774   Grant Book M, page 781

100 acres bounded on all sides by vacant land.

****

Cade, Robert
300 acres in St. George Parish

Granted on June 2, 1767   Grant Book F, page 266

300 acres bounded on all sides by vacant land.

****

Camford, Jeremiah
250 acres in St. George Parish

Granted on July 5, 1774   Grant Book M, page 19

250 acres bounded on the north by Thomas Yarborough and on
all other sides by vacant land.

****

Camp, William
300 acres in St. George Parish

Granted on July 1, 1760   Grant Book C, page 302

300 acres bounded on the south by Bryan Creek, west by
William Green and on all other sides by vacant land.

****

Cannon, David
100 acres in St. George Parish

Granted on August 2, 1774   Grant Book M, page 170

100 acres bounded on all sides by vacant land.

****

Cannon, David
200 acres in St. George Parish

Surveyed on June 25, 1773   Plat Book M, page 44
Granted on August 2, 1774   Grant Book M, page 175

200 acres bounded on the southwest by Sarah Underwood, George
Walker and James Nicols, northwest by Thomas Lewis, Rev. Mr.
Lowten and Thomas Yarborough and northeast by Thomas Lewis
and Briar Creek.

****

Capers, Richard
300 acres in St. George Parish

Granted on January 3, 1775   Grant Book M, page 865

300 acres bounded on the southwest by Breazell and vacant
land, northeast by William O'Bryan and southeast by the
Great Ogechee River.

****

Carey, Alexander
100 acres in St. George Parish

Recorded June 17, 1773   Grant Book I, page 934

100 acres in Queensborough Township bounded on all sides by
vacant land and also Lot49 in the Town of Queensborough.

****

Carrington, Richard
250 acres in St. George Parish

Granted on July 7, 1767   Grant Book F, page 287

250 acres bounded on the east by James Stiggans and on all
other sides by vacant land.

****

Carter, James
350 acres in St. George Parish

Granted on October 2, 1764   Grant Book E, page 40

350 acres located at McIntoshes Swamp and bounded on all
sides by vacant land.

****

Cary, John
400 acres in St. George Parish

Granted on November 6, 1770   Grant Book I, page 209

Lot 2 in Town of Queensborough and also 400 acres in the
Township of Queensborough bounded on all sides by vacant land.

****

Case, William
200 acres in St. George Parish

Granted on August 3, 1762   Grant Book D, page 172

200 acres bounded on the northeast by Bryan Creek, west by John Emanuel and on all other sides by vacant land.

****

Castillow, James
300 acres in St. George Parish

Granted on June 5, 1771   Grant Book I, page 336

300 acres bounded on all sides by vacant land.

****

Cater, Edward
200 acres in St. George Parish

Granted on August 1, 1769   Grant Book G, page 382

200 acres bounded on all sides by vacant land.

****

Cater, Edward
100 acres in St. George Parish

Granted on December 3, 1771   Grant Book I, page 469

100 acres bounded on the northeast by Stephen---, southeast by James Ogilvie, partly on the northeast by ----Radcliffe and on the southwest by vacant land.

****

Cattlett, John
200 acres in St. George Parish

Granted on August 4, 1767   Grant Book F, page 311

200 acres bounded on the southeast by William Moore and on all other sides by vacant land.

****

Catlett, John
100 acres in St. George Parish

Granted on June 7, 1774   Grant Book I, page 1044

100 acres bounded on the north and east by his own land and
on the west by Joseph Gresham's land.

****

Caudery, Thomas
200 acres in St. George Parish

Granted on April 3, 1764   Grant Book D, page 409

200 acres bounded on the southwest by William Mainer, northeast by William Handley and on the northwest by John Burnsides.

****

Cavanah, Charles
100 acres in St. George Parish

Surveyed on January 30, 1767   Plat Book C, page 313

100 acres originally surveyed for John Sellers, thence ordered
to Charles Cavanah on February 5, 1771. See above Plat
Book reference.

****

Cavenah, Arthur
100 acres in St. George Parish

Granted on April 6, 1773   Grant Book I, page 938

100 acres bounded on all sides by vacant land.

****

Cavenah, David
100 acres in St. George Parish

Granted on October 29, 1765   Grant Book E. page 405

100 acres bounded on all sides by vacant land.

****

Cavenah, David
150 acres in St. George Parish

Granted on June 6, 1769   Grant Book G, page 326

150 acres bounded on all sides by vacant land.

****

Cavenah, David
100 acres in St. George Parish

Granted on August 2, 1774   Grant Book M, page 172

100 acres bounded on the southeast by the said David Cavenah
and on all other sides by vacant land.

****

Cavenah, Henry
100 acres in St. George Parish

Granted on August 5, 1766   Grant Book E, page 329

100 acres bounded on all sides by vacant land.

****

Cavenah, Henry
100 acres in St. George Parish

Granted on November 1, 1774   Grant Book M, page 633

100 acres bounded on the southwest by land called the Dutch
Survey, north by land ordered Robert Cade and on all other
sides by vacant land.

****

Cavenah, Nicholas
300 acres in St. George Parish

Surveyed on March 14, 1764   Plat Book M, page 24
Granted on October 29, 1765   Grant Book E, page 252

300 acres located on the south side of Buckhead upon the
Great Ogechee River at a place called the Spring Branch.

****

Cavenah, Nicholas
150 acres in St. George Parish

Surveyed on July 16, 1765   Plat Book M, page 24
Granted on October 31, 1765   Grant Book E, page 296

150 acres bounded on the east by the said Nicholas Cavenah
and on all other sides by vacant land.

****

Cawdry, Thomas
200 acres in St. George Parish

Surveyed on August 14, 1759   Plat Book C, page 36

Original warrant states that the land is located on the south
side of Brier Creek on Boggy Branch near Spencer's Cowpen.

****

Cawthorn, William Dabney
200 acres in St. George Parish

Surveyed on June 6, 1759   Plat Book C, page 35

200 acres bounded on the northeast by the Savannah River and
on the northwest by John Rae.

****

Cherry, Nathan
200 acres in St. George Parish

Granted on March 3, 1767   Grant Book F, page 99

200 acres bounded on the northeast by Roger Lawson and on all
other sides by vacant land.

****

Chestnut, Alexander
300 acres in St. George Parish

Granted on November 6, 1770   Grant Book I, page 210

Lot 3 in Town of Queensborough and also 300 acres in the
Township of Queensborough.

****

Chisolm, Thomas
100 acres in St. George Parish

Granted on August 2, 1774   Grant Book M, page 166

100 acres bounded on all sides by vacant land.

****

Churchill, Charles
100 acres in St. George Parish

Granted on November 1, 1774   Grant Book M, page 640

100 acres bounded on the southwest by William Wylly and on
all other sides by vacant land.

****

Clark and McGilivray
50 acres in St. George Parish

Surveyed on May 18, 1758   Plat Book C, page 400

50 acres bounded on the southwest by Bryer Creek and on all
other sides by vacant land.

****

Clark, Christopher
250 acres in St. George Parish

Original survey date unknown
Resurveyed on March 6, 1847   Plat Book M, page 131
Granted on June 5, 1770   Grant Book I, page 19

250 acres bounded on the northeast by John Fitch and resurveyed
for Sarah and Christopher Clark, grandchildren of Christopher
Clar, and found to contain 265 acres.

****

Clark, John
200 acres in St. George Parish

Surveyed on April 2, 1758   Plat Book C, page 35

33

200 acres bounded on the southwest by Briar Creek. The original warrant states, "200 acres upon the north side of Briar Creek about six miles from Savannah River bounded on all sides by vacant land.

****

Clark, Lucy
150 acres in St. George Parish

Granted on November 5, 1771   Grant Book I, page 450

150 acres bounded on all sides by vacant land.

****

Clark, Lucy
150 acres in St. George Parish

Granted on October 6, 1772   Grant Book I, page 779

150 acres bounded on the northeast by ----Lindsey and on all other sides by vacant land.

****

Clark, Samuel
150 acres in St. George Parish

Granted on August 1, 1769   Grant Book G, page 381

150 acres bounded on the northwest by Andrew Berryhill and on all other sides by vacant land.

****

Clark, Samuel
250 acres in St. George Parish

Granted on March 2, 1773   Grant Book I, page 913

250 acres bounded on the northwest by Josiah Adams and on all other sides by vacant land.

****

Clark, Sarah
250 acres in St. George Parish

34

Original survey date unknown
Resurveyed on March 6, 1847   Plat Book M, page 131
Granted on June 5, 1770   Grant Book I, page 19

Granted to Christopher Clark and bounded on the northeast
by John Fitch. Resurveyed for Sarah and Christopher Clark,
grandchildren of Christopher Clark and found to contain
265 acres.

****

Clebborn, Joshua
500 acres in St. George Parish

Original survey date unknown
Resurveyed on May 19, 1829   Plat Book M, page 124
Granted on July 5, 1774   Grant Book M, page 97

Granted to James Read and James Deveaux in trust for
William Handley, 500 acres bounded on the south by ----Pray,
west by Helvenstine and east by Bledsoe. Resurveyed for
Joshua Clebborn and found to contain 378 acres.

****

Clements, Jacob
100 acres in St. George Parish

Granted on September 6, 1774   Grant Book M, page 294

100 acres bounded on the north by William Williams and on all
other sides by vacant land.

****

Clements, Jacob
200 acres in St. George Parish

Granted on September 6, 1774   Grant Book M, page 295

200 acres bounded on the north by William Williams and on
all other sides by vacant land.

****

Clements, Samuel
550 acres in St. George Parish

Granted on September 6, 1774   Grant Book M, page 296

550 acres in Queensborough Township bounded on the west by Adam Morrison, northeast by James Blair, southwest by Walker Stevenson and southeast by John Ingram and John Morrison.

****

Clifton, Sarah
100 acres in St. George Parish

Granted on October 4, 1774   Grant Book M, page 425

100 acres bounded on the northwest by John Rae and on all other sides by vacant land.

****

Coburn, John
100 acres in St. George Parish

Granted on March 1, 1768   Grant Book G, page 42

100 acres bounded on the northwest by John Sellers and on the southwest by Henry Cavenah.

****

Cochran, John
100 acres in St. George Parish

Granted on September 3, 1771   Grant Book I, page 401

100 acres bounded on the north---by Briar Creek and on all other sides by vacant land.

****

Cock, Zebulon
200 acres in St. George Parish

Granted on August 6, 1771   Grant Book I, page 379

200 acres bounded on the east by Jethro Roundtree and on all other sides by vacant land.

****

Cockran, William
200 acres in St. George Parish

Surveyed on August 10, 1759   Plat Book C, page 36

200 acres bounded on the northeast by Thomas Bell and on the
northwest by the Savannah River. Original warrant states,
"located about 5 miles above Stoney Bluff in the district
of Halifax on the Savannah River.

****

Colson, Sanders
150 acres in St. George Parish

Surveyed on September 16, 1768   Plat Book M, page 65
Granted on February 7, 1769   Grant Book G, page 266

150 acres bounded on the west by John Fletcher and on the
east by Sanders Colson.

****

Colson, William
250 acres in St. George Parish

Granted on April 13, 1761   Grant Book C, page 109

250 acres in Halifax District bounded on the south by Steigol
and on the north by Nathaniel Miller.

****

Colson, William
100 acres in St. George Parish

Granted on January 1, 1765   Grant Book E, page 97

100 acres located near a place called Horse Creek and bounded
on all sides by vacant land.

****

Colson, William
150 acres in St. George and St. Matthew Parish

Granted on August 6, 1765   Grant Book E, page 211

150 acres located 60 miles from Savannah and bounded on the south by Nathaniel Miller and vacant land and on the east by Abraham Lundy.

****

Conyers, John
200 acres in St. George Parish

Granted on April 13, 1761   Grant Book D, page 367

200 acres bounded on the southeast by John Brunson and on all other sides by vacant land.

****

Conyers, John
300 acres in St. George Parish

Survey date not given   Plat Book M, page 114
Granted on April 3, 1764   Grant Book D, page 410

300 acres bounded on all sides by vacant land.

****

Conyers, John
50 acres in St. George Parish

Granted on June 6, 1769   Grant Book H, page 25

50 acres bounded on the southeast by land of the said grantee, northwest by Benjamin Williamson and northeast by --- Blyth.

****

Cooper, Robert
450 acres in St. George Parish

Granted on April 2, 1771   Grant Book I, page 298

450 acres in Queensborough Township bounded on the southeast by John Kennedy and on the southeast by a creek, and also Lot 4 in the Town of Queensborough.

****

Cooper, Robert
50 acres in St. George Parish

38

Surveyed on April 1, 1771   Plat Book M, page 23

50 acres bounded on the east and northeast by the said
Robert Cooper and on the west by Lamberts Creek.

****

Coughlan, John
200 acres in St. George Parish

Granted on July 2, 1765   Grant Book E, page 184

200 acres bounded on the north by Briar Creek and on all
other sides by vacant land.

****

Coulson, Jacob
100 acres in St. George Parish

Surveyed on January 12, 1758   Plat Book C, page 35

100 acres bounded on the west by Briar Creek and on all
other sides by vacant land.

****

Coulson, Thomas
250 acres in St. George and St. Matthew Parish

Granted on October 6, 1767   Grant Book F, page 377

250 acres bounded on the east by John Haruage and on all
other sides by vacant land.

****

Cowper, Basil
150 acres in St. George Parish

Granted on March 4, 1771   Grant Book I, page 265

Granted to Basil Cowper, William Telfair and Edward Telfair
and bounded on all sides by vacant land.

****

Cowper, Henry
200 acres in St. George Parish

Granted on June 7, 1774   Grant Book I, page 1057

200 acres bounded on the south by Samuel Holton and on all other sides by vacant land.

****

Cowper, Samuel
100 acres in St. George Parish

Granted on July 7, 1772   Grant Book I, page 681

100 acres bounded on all sides by vacant land. ·

****

Cox, Caleb
100 acres in St. George Parish

Granted on May 2, 1769   Grant Book G, page 313

100 acres bounded on the northeast by James Bickham and on all other sides by vacant land.

****

Cox, John H.
200 acres in St. George Parish

Original survey date unknown
Resurveyed on February 16, 1836   Plat Book M, page 129
Granted on November 1, 1774   Grant Book M, page 760

Originally granted to Thomas Hamilton but resurveyed for John H. Cox and found to contain 225 acres.

****

Cressup, Moses
250 acres in St. George Parish

Granted on December 6, 1768   Grant Book G, page 227

250 acres bounded on the northwest by Barrett Montgomery and on the northeast by Thomas Lewis.

****

Crissop, Moses
250 acres in St. George Parish

40

Granted on June 7, 1768   Grant Book G, page 119

250 acres bounded on the southeast by Charles Gee and on all other sides by vacant land.

****

Cromby, Robert
150 acres in St. George Parish

Granted on August 2, 1774   Grant Book M, page 174

150 acres in Queensborough, bounded on the southwest by David Wood and on all other sides by vacant land.

****

Crossley, William
850 acres in St. George Parish

Granted on March 1, 1768   Grant Book G, page 44

850 acres bounded on the west by Lamberts Big Creek and on the southwest by land ordered David Holmes.

****

Croswell, James
200 acres in St. George Parish

Surveyed on October 22, 1768   Plat Book C, page 36

200 acres bounded on the north by John McNiss and John Bruman and on all other sides by vacant land.

****

Crumb, Henry
500 acres in St. George Parish

Granted on February 2, 1768   Grant Book G, page 20

500 acres bounded on the south by John Strayton, west by William Ducker and east by Henry Crumb.

****

Cutrell, Amos
200 acres in St. George Parish

Granted on April 7, 1767   Grant Book F, page 167

200 acres bounded on the east by Philip Howell and on all other sides by vacant land.

****

Darby, John
100 acres in St. George Parish

Granted on November 6, 1770   Grant Book I, page 207

100 acres in Queensborough Township and bounded on all sides by vacant land.

****

D'Arcy, Joseph
250 acres in St. George Parish

Granted on October 3, 1769   Grant Book G, page 429

250 acres bounded on all sides by vacant land.

****

David, Neal
200 acres in St. George Parish

Surveyed on October 24, 1764   Plat Book M, page 33
Granted on May 5, 1767   Grant Book F, page 226

200 acres bounded on the north by Lachlan McGillivray, east by Douglass and Pettygrew.

****

Davis, Francis
50 acres in St. George Parish

Granted on June 7, 1774   Grant Book H, page 103

50 acres bounded on the northwest by George Harnage and on all other sides by vacant land.

****

Davis, John
150 acres in St. George Parish

Granted on August 2, 1774   Grant Book M, page 177

150 acres bounded on the northwest by John Gasper Griner, southwest by Briar Creek and southeast by William Williams.

****

Davis, John
200 acres in St. George Parish

Granted on September 6, 1774   Grant Book M, page 301

200 acres bounded on all sides by vacant land.

****

Davis, John
50 acres in St. George Parish

Surveyed on December 22, 1758   Plat Book C, page 58

Original warrant states the tract is located near the Spaniards Cabbin adjoining the 150 acres heretofore granted John Davis, on the west.

****

Davis, Myrick
150 acres in St. George Parish

Granted on August 2, 1774   Grant Book M, page 181

150 acres bounded on the northeast by Thomas Ford and on the northwest by Jacob Lewis.

****

Davis, Samuel
300 acres in St. George Parish

Granted on October 3, 1769   Grant Book G, page 427

300 acres bounded on all sides by vacant land.

****

Davis, Samuel
100 acres in St. George Parish

Granted on April 6, 1773   Grant Book I, page 937

100 acres bounded on all sides by vacant land.

****

Davis, Thomas
100 acres in St. Georgia Parish

Granted on September 2, 1766   Grant Book E, page 354

100 acres bounded on the northeast by Great Ogechee River,
on the northwest by Martin Dasher, on the southeast by
Mathew Zettler.

****

Davis, William
200 acres in St. George Parish

Granted on December 6, 1768   Grant Book G, page 228

200 acres bounded on all sides by vacant land.

****

Dean, Ether
200 acres in St. George Parish

Granted on January 19, 1773   Grant Book I, page 848

200 acres bounded on all sides by vacant land.

****

Dean, Luke
75 acres in St. George Parish

Granted on October 29, 1765   Grant Book E, page 254

75 acres bounded on all sides by vacant land.

****

Debutts, John Collins
200 acres in St. George Parish

Granted on October 4, 1774   Grant Book M, page 431

200 acres bounded on the southeast by Isaac Heaton.
****

Deerman, William
100 acres in St. George Parish

Granted on January 3, 1775   Grant Book M, page 867

100 acres bounded on the west by Kincade and Sharp, east
by Robert Douglass and northeast by Daniel O'Sheal.

****

Dell, Philip
250 acres in St. George Parish

Granted on June 5, 1770   Grant Book I, page 20

250 acres heretofore ordered to and surveyed for James
Nesmith and bounded on the northeast by the Savannah River
and southeast by William Lin.

****

Dell, Philip
100 acres in St. George Parish

Granted on June 5, 1770   Grant Book I, page 21

100 acres heretofore ordered to and surveyed for William
Linden and bounded on the northeast by the Savannah River
northwest by James Nesmith and southeast by John Eito.

****

Denison, Patrick
350 acres in St. George Parish

Granted on November 6, 1770   Grant Book I, page 180

350 acres bounded on all sides by vacant land.

****

Read, James and James DeVeaux, in trust for William Handley
500 acres in St. George Parish

Original survey date unknown
Resurveyed on May 19, 1829   Plat Book M, page 124
Granted on July 5, 1774   Grant Book M, page 97

500 acres bounded on the south by ---Pray, west by Helvenstine,
east by Bledsoe. Resurveyed in 1829 for Joshua Cleborn for 378
acres.

Deveaux, James and James Read in trust for William Handley
500 acres in St. George Parish

Granted on July 5, 1774   Grant Book M, page 98

500 acres bounded on the northwest by Nunes and John Lott
and on all other sides by vacant land.

****

Deverixzo, Michael
100 acres in St. George Parish

Granted on February 7, 1775   Grant Book M, page 990

100 acres bounded on all sides by vacant land.

****

Deverixzo, Peter
100 acres in St. George Parish

Granted on February 7, 1775   Grant Book M, page 989

100 acres bounded on all sides by vacant land.

****

Deverixzo, Stephen
100 acres in St. George Parish

Granted on February 7, 1775   Grant Book M, page 988

100 acres bounded on all sides by vacant land.

****

Dickson, John
200 acres in St. George Parish

Granted on August 2, 1774   Grant Book M, page 180

200 acres bounded on the southwest by Josiah Roberts and
Downey and on the southeast by William Downey.

****

Dill, Philip
100 acres in St. George Parish

Surveyed on November 7, 1759   Plat Book C, page 143

Surveyed for William Lindon, thence ordered to Philip Dill on April 3, 1770. Bounded on the northeast by the Savannah River, northwest by James Nothsmith and southeast by John Kitts. See grant to Philip Dell, Grant Book I, page 21.

****

Dodd, John
100 acres in St. George Parish

Surveyed on February 18, 1773   Plat Book C, page 57

100 acres bounded on the northwest by Failey and on the east by Sharp.

****

Dohart, John
100 acres in St. George Parish

Surveyed on August 10, 1759   Plat Book C, page 55

Original warrant states, "100 acres on the North Fork of Walnut Branch on the south side of Brier Creek a quarter of a Mile above John Nelson's land."

****

Donelson, John
250 acres in St. George Parish

Granted on September 6, 1774   Grant Book M, page 305

250 acres in Queensborough bounded on the southeast by Chevers Creek and on all other sides by vacant land.

****

Douglas, Daniel
100 acres in St. George Parish

Granted on February 5, 1765   Grant Book E, page 109

100 acres bounded on the south by Thomas Irwin, northwest by David Emanuel and northeast by James Houston.

****

Douglass, Daniel
150 acres in St. George Parish

Original survey date unknown
Resurveyed on February 6, 1838   Plat Book M, page 129
Granted on March 3, 1767   Grant Book F, page 105

150 acres bounded on the south by the Great Ogechee River,
southeast by the said Daniel Douglass. Resurveyed for
Augustus H. Anderson.

****

Douglass, Daniel
150 acres in St. George Parish

Granted on April 5, 1768   Grant Book G, page 71

150 acres bounded on the south by Richard Scruggs and on
all other sides by vacant land.

****

Douglass, Daniel
150 acres in St. George Parish

Granted on March 6, 1770   Grant Book G, page 543

150 acres bounded on the southwest by James Houston, southeast
by Richard Scruggs and Daniel Douglass and northwest by
James Bowie and vacant land.

****

Douglass, Daniel
150 acres in St. George Parish

Granted on May 5, 1772   Grant Book I, page 582

150 acres bounded on the northeast by Thomas Irwin, and
on the northwest by Peter Elliott and Thomas Ford.

****

Douglass, David
500 acres in St. George Parish

Granted on July 7, 1761   Grant Book C, page 148

500 acres bounded on the east by the Savannah River and on the north by Lachlan McGillavray.

****

Douglass, John
600 acres in St. George Parish

Granted on November 1, 1774   Grant Book M, page 650

600 acres bounded on the northeast by Briar Creek, northwest by Nicholas Horton, south by Johnson and Wylly and William Colson.

****

Douglass, Michael
250 acres in St. George Parish

Granted on September 6, 1774   Grant Book M, page 306

250 acres bounded on the southeast and northeast by ----- Minsey, northwest by Thomas Shruder and Jesse Brasher.

****

Douglass, Robert
100 acres in St. George Parish

Granted on October 6, 1772   Grant Book I, page 770

100 acres bounded on the southeast by granted land and on the southwest by ----Sharp.

****

Douglass, Samuel
500 acres in St. George Parish

Granted on July 5, 1774   Grant Book M, page 23

500 acres bounded on the east by Edward Hill, on the south by Brown and on the west by Isaac Perry.

****

Douglass, Samuel
500 acres in St. George Parish

Granted on October 4, 1774   Grant Book M, page 426

500 acres bounded on the northeast by the said Samuel Douglass and on all other sides by vacant land.

****

Douglass, Samuel
500 acres in St. George Parish

Granted on October 4, 1774   Grant Book M, page 427

500 acres bounded on the northeast by Seth Slocumb and vacant land and southwest by the said Samuel Douglass.

****

Downey, William
300 acres in St. George Parish

Granted on May 5, 1767   Grant Book F, page 227

300 acres bounded on all sides by vacant land.

****

Ducker, William
150 acres in St. George Parish

Granted on July 3, 1764   Grant Book E, page 20

150 acres bounded on the north by Buckhead Creek and east by James Pugh.

****

Duglass, Daniel
150 acres in St. George Parish

Granted on October 29, 1765   Grant Book E, page 297

150 acres bounded on all sides by vacant land.

****

Duhart, John
100 acres in St. George Parish

Granted on May 5, 1767   Grant Book F, page 225

100 acres bounded on the east by the said John Duhart.

****

Dumvill, Robert
150 acres in St. George Parish

Granted on May 7, 1771   Grant Book I, page 306

150 acres in Queensborough Township bounded on the southwest by Crosby, northeast by John Kennedy and southeast by Robert Cooper.

****

Dundas, Ralph
500 acres in St. George Parish

Surveyed on August 1, 1774   Plat Book C, page 55

500 acres bounded on the northeast by the said Ralph Dundas, northwest by James Maxwell and southwest by John Large.

****

Dundas, Ralph
500 acres in St. George Parish

Surveyed on August 1, 1774   Plat Book C, page 56

500 acres bounded on the southwest by the said Ralph Dundas.

****

Dundas, Ralph
500 acres in St. George Parish

Surveyed on July 26, 1774   Plat Book C, page 55

500 acres bounded on the northwest by Josiah Tattnall, northeast by Jonathon Kemp, Daniel Underwood and Sarah Underwood.

****

Dundas, Ralph
1000 acres in St. George Parish

Surveyed on August 4, 1774   Plat Book C, page 55

1000 acres bounded on the southwest by the Augusta Road and on all other sides by vacant land.

****

Dundas, Ralph
500 acres in St. George Parish

Surveyed on August 1, 1774   Loose original plat

Original warrant says, "unto Ralph Dundas agreeable to his
Majesty's Royal Bounty and Proclamation, 500 acres in St.
George Parish near land surveyed for the Revd Timothy
Lowton dec.^{d} in lieu of like quantity formerly ordered him
but not surveyed."

****

Dundas, Ralph
500 acres in St. George Parish

Warrant dated January 28, 1774

Original warrant states,"unto Ralph Dundas agreeable to his
Majesty's Royal Bounty and Proclamation 500 acres in St.
George Parish near land of Thomas Fusil on Briar Creek in
lieu of the like quantity formerly ordered him but not
surveyed."

****

Dunlap, Joseph
150 acres in St. George Parish

Granted on September 3, 1765   Grant Book E, page 229

150 acres bounded on the north by Jacob Collson and on all
other sides by vacant land.

****

Earle, John
300 acres in St. George Parish

Granted on November 1, 1774   Grant Book M, page 652

300 acres bounded on the northeast by Thomas Yarborough,
Jeremiah Cramford and John Sharp, northwest by Reverend
Mr. Louten and southwest by Robe.

****

Eason, George
200 acres in St. George Parish

Granted on April 6, 1773   Grant Book I, page 940

200 acres bounded on the southeast and the northeast by Fitzgerald and on the northwest by Benjamin Richardson.

****

Eastlake, Samuel
100 acres in St. George Parish

Granted on July 7, 1767   Grant Book F, page 292

100 acres bounded on the south by Beaver Dam Creek, northwest by John Goode and northeast by land ordered to the said Samuel Eastlake.

****

Eastlake, Samuel
150 acres in St. George Parish

Granted on July 7, 1767   Grant Book F, page 293

150 acres bounded on the south by Beaver Dam Creek, east by John Lott, southwest by land ordered to the said Samuel Eastlake and northwest by John Goode.

****

Elbert, Samuel
50 acres in St. George Parish

Granted on June 7, 1774   Grant Book H, page 104

50 acres bounded on all sides by vacant land.

****

Elbert, Samuel
100 acres in St. George Parish

Granted on January 7, 1772   Grant Book I, page 492

100 acres bounded on all sides by vacant land.

****

Elbert, Samuel
100 acres in St. George Parish

Granted on April 6, 1773   Grant Book I, page 939

100 acres bounded on all sides by vacant land.

****

Elbert, Samuel
100 acres in St. George Parish

Granted on June 7, 1774   Grant Book I, page 1090

100 acres bounded partly on the west by land of the said
Samuel Elbert, east near land of John Rae, deceased and on
all other sides by vacant land.

****

Elbert, Samuel
150 acres in St. George Parish

Granted on November 1, 1774   Grant Book M, page 725

150 acres bounded on the northeast by Edmund Pearce and
vacant land, southwest by Arthur Wall and west by Isaac
Perry. See Robert Rae.

****

Elbert, Samuel
391 acres in St. George Parish

Granted on December 6, 1774   Grant Book M, page 824

391 acres bounded on the northwest by land ordered David
Cavenah, southeast by unknown land, northeast by vacant
land and southwest by the Great Ogechee River. See Robert
Rae.

****

Elbert, Samuel
109 acres in St. George Parish

Granted on December 6, 1774   Grant Book M, page 825

109 acres bounded on the east by John Rae, north by ---
Robinson and on the southeast by Briar Creek. See Robert
Rae.

****

Elliott, Grey
1000 acres in St. George Parish

Granted on August 4, 1772   Grant Book I, page 703

1000 acres bounded partly on the northwest by Nathan Hooker
and on all other sides by vacant land.

****

Elliott, William
150 acres in St. George Parish

Granted on June 5, 1771   Grant Book I, page 337

150 acres bounded on the northeast by John Reeves, west by
land laid out for a Church and south by Isaac Lindsey.

****

Elphinson, Philip
300 acres in St. George Parish

No date for original survey
Resurveyed on July 20, 1791   Plat Book M, page 9
Granted on April 6, 1773   Grant Book I, page 943

300 acres bounded on the south by John Higdon and David
Green, partly on the north by George Galphin and on all other
sides by vacant land. When resurveyed in 1791, 149 acres
were surveyed for Thomas Jones and 151 acres for Daniel
Evans.

****

Emanuel, Amos
150 acres in St. George Parish

Granted on June 6, 1769   Grant Book G, page 328

150 acres bounded on all sides by vacant land.

****

Emanuel, Amos
200 acres in St. George Parish

Granted on June 5, 1771   Grant Book I, page 338

200 acres bounded on the west by Samuel Boykin and on the east by John Emanuel.

****

Emanuel, Assa
100 acres in St. George Parish

Granted on August 6, 1771   Grant Book I, page 382

100 acres bounded on the southeast and partly on the southwest by Hall Hudson, northeast by William Case and on all other sides by vacant land.

****

Emanuel, David
200 acres in St. George Parish

Surveyed on July 8, 1757   Plat Book C, page 59
Granted on December 7, 1762   Grant Book D, page 262

200 acres in the District of Halifax, bounded on the east by James Houstoun. Original warrant states, "200 acres on the south side of Bryer Creek joining James Hutson's land."

****

Emanuel, David
200 acres in St. George Parish

Granted on May 7, 1765   Grant Book E, page 154

200 acres bounded on all sides by vacant land.

****

Emanuel, David, Jr.
100 acres in St. George Parish

Granted on March 3, 1767   Grant Book F, page 108

100 acres bounded on all sides by vacant land.

****

Eppinger, John
250 acres in St. George Parish

Granted on January 2, 1770   Grant Book G, page 498

250 acres bounded on the southeast by Randall Bracey and on
all other sides by vacant land.

****

Evans, Daniel
300 acres in St. George Parish

No date for original survey
Resurveyed on July 20, 1791   Plat Book M, page 9
Granted on April 6, 1773   Grant Book I, page 943

Originally granted to Philip Elphinson but when resurveyed
in 1791, 149 acres were surveyed for Thomas Jones and 151
acres for Daniel Evans. The 300 acres were bounded on the
south by John Higdon and David Green, partly on the north
by George Galphin and on all other sides by vacant land.

****

Ewen, William
500 acres in St. George Parish

Surveyed on November 17, 1760   Plat Book C, page 58
Granted on November 3, 1761   Grant Book C, page 273

500 acres bounded on the northeast and southeast by Lachlan
McGillavray and the plat shows it was bounded on the
northeast by the Savannah River. Original warrant states,
"500 acres on purchase laying on Savannah River bounded
southerly by a tract of 1000 acres granted Lachlan McGillivray."

****

Ewen, William
500 acres in St. George Parish

Granted on November 1, 1774   Grant Book M, page 651

500 acres bounded on the northeast by the Ogechee River,
southeast by land ordered to William Maxwell, southwest
by vacant land and northwest by land supposed to be
Samuel Savery's land and vacant land.

****

Falsom, Laurence
150 acres in St. George Parish

Granted on November 1, 1774   Grant Book M, page 654

150 acres bounded on all sides by vacant land.

****

Faming, Joachim Noel
150 acres in St. George Parish

Granted on May 4, 1773   Grant Book I, page 973

150 acres bounded on all sides by vacant land.

****

Fenn, Zachariah
250 acres in St. George Parish

Granted on July 2, 1765   Grant Book E, page 190

250 acres bounded on the east by the Savannah River, south
by a creek in McBeans Swamp and north by John Pettygrew.

****

Fenn, Zachariah
300 acres in St. George Parish

Granted on December 1, 1767   Grant Book F, page 420

300 acres bounded on the east by the said Zachariah Fenn and
on all other sides by vacant land.

****

Fenn, Zachariah
1000 acres in St. George and St. Paul Parish

Granted on April 7, 1772   Grant Book I, page 550

1000 acres bounded on the north and east by John Rae and land of
Zachariah Fenn, southeast by land ordered to Philip Alston, and
west by land surveyed for the said Zachariah Fenn.

****

Finch, George
200 acres in St. George Parish

Granted on November 1, 1774   Grant Book M, page 657

200 acres bounded on the southwest by Briar Creek and on the northwest by Thomas Frederick.

****

Finlay, James
300 acres in St. George Parish

Granted on January 5, 1773   Grant Book I, page 829

300 acres in the Township of Queensborough bounded on the west by Patrick Dennison and also lot 12 in the Town of Queensborough.

****

Finley, James
200 acres in St. George Parish

Granted on October 4, 1774   Grant Book M, page 439

200 acres in Queensborough bounded on the northeast by William McConkey, northwest by John Darby and southwest by John Cary.

****

Fisher, Nicholas
200 acres in St. George Parish

Granted on May 1, 1764   Grant Book E, page 10

200 acres bounded on the northeast by the Savannah River, south by William Scolson, north by George Strigel and west by vacant land.

****

Fisher, Nicholas
100 acres in St. George Parish

Granted on February 3, 1767   Grant Book F, page 60

100 acres bounded on the northwest by James Roberts.

****

Fitch, John
100 acres in St. George Parish

Surveyed on March 16, 1759   Plat Book C, page 62

100 acres bounded on the northwest by Spirit Creek and
James Parris and southwest by John Fitch. Original
warrant states, "100 acres on Spirit Creek adjoining 300
acres there last granted him."

****

Fitzgerald, James
200 acres in St. George Parish

Granted on March 6, 1770   Grant Book G, page 548

200 acres bounded on the northwest by Dukes Pond and on all
other sides by vacant land.

****

Fitzgerald, James
100 acres in St. George Parish

Granted on January 3, 1775   Grant Book M, page 874

100 acres bounded on all sides by vacant land.

****

Fleeming, John
100 acres in St. George Parish

Granted on September 6, 1774   Grant Book M, page 309

100 acres bounded on the southwest by Robert Rogers, northwest by vacant land and northeast by Lamberts Creek.

****

Fleeting, Richard
200 acres in St. George Parish

Granted on August 2, 1774   Grant Book M, page 184

200 acres bounded on the south by Great Ogechee River, east by
Reedy Branch and land of David Grier and Glebe land, north by
David Grier and vacant land and west by Patrick McKay and vacant.

****

Fleming, James
100 acres in St. George Parish

Granted on April 2, 1771   Grant Book I, page 299

100 acres in Queensborough Township and also lot 6 in the
Town of Queensborough.

****

Fleming, Samuel
350 acres in St. George Parish

Granted on July 3, 1770   Grant Book I, page 93

350 acres in the Township of Queensborough and also lot
66 in the Town of Queensborough.

****

Fletcher, James
100 acres in St. George Parish

Surveyed on March 21, 1764   Plat Book M, page 66
Granted on March 5, 1765   Grant Book E, page 123

100 acres bounded on the west by Walker's Spring Branch and
on all other sides by vacant land.

****

Fletcher, James
100 acres in St. George Parish

Granted on March 3, 1767   Grant Book F, page 111

100 acres bounded on the south by the said James Fletcher
and on all other sides by vacant land.

****

Fletcher, James
100 acres in St. George Parish

Surveyed on November 16, 1765   Plat Book M, page 66
Granted on August 7, 1770   Grant Book I, page 70

100 acres bounded on the northeast by the said grantee.

****

Folson, Jeremiah
250 acres in St. George Parish

Granted on January 3, 1775   Grant Book M, page 872

250 acres bounded on all sides by vacant land.

****

Ford, Thomas
100 acres in St. George Parish

Granted on October 29, 1765   Grant Book E, page 293

100 acres bounded on the northwest by Peter Elliott and all other sides by vacant land.

****

Ford, Thomas
100 acres in St. George Parish

Granted on February 6, 1770   Grant Book G, page 522

100 acres bounded on all sides by vacant land.

****

Forrester, Stephen
300 acres in St. George Parish

Granted on February 5, 1771   Grant Book I, page 247

300 acres bounded on the north by McBeans Creek and on all other sides by vacant land.

****

Fox, James
300 acres in St. George Parish

Granted on April 7, 1772   Grant Book I, page 552

300 acres bounded on the northeast by Thomas Irvin and on the southwest by Rocky Comfort Creek.

****

Fox, William
100 acres in St. George Parish

Granted on August 1, 1769   Grant Book G, page 386

100 acres bounded on the west by Dry Branch and on all
other sides by vacant land.

****

Francis, Frederick
300 acres in St. George Parish

Granted on May 5, 1772   Grant Book I, page 586

300 acres bounded on the east by Thomas Red and William
Newberry and on the northwest by John Henderson.

****

Fraser, Donald
100 acres in St. George Parish

Granted on January 6, 1767   Grant Book F, page 19

100 acres bounded on the southwest by Briar Creek.

****

Frederick, Thomas
200 acres in St. George Parish

Granted on July 5, 1774   Grant Book M, page 33

200 acres bounded on the southwest by Briar Creek.

****

Freeman, John
100 acres in St. George Parish

Granted on July 5, 1774   Grant Book M, page 35

100 acres bounded on the southwest by Bagley, northwest
by Vaught and on the northeast by Briar Creek.

****

Fryer, John
150 acres in St. George Parish

Surveyed on August 15, 1759   Plat Book C, pages 297, 424
Granted on July 2, 1765   Grant Book E, page 183

150 acres located 104 miles from Savannah and bounded on the northeast by the Savannah River. Originally surveyed for William Sissin, thence regranted to John Fryer by order of October 2, 1764.

****

Fulton, John
100 acres in St. George Parish

Granted on May 4, 1773   Grant Book I, page 974

100 acres bounded on the northeast by the said John Fulton.

****

Fusil, Thomas
150 acres in St. George Parish

Granted on May 5, 1767   Grant Book F, page 228

150 acres bounded on the west by Paul Harrold.

****

Fusil, Thomas
75 acres in St. George Parish

Granted on May 2, 1769   Grant Book H, page 23

75 acres bounded on all sides by vacant land.

****

Fusill, Moses
100 acres in St. George Parish

Granted on December 4, 1770   Grant Book I, page 217

100 acres bounded on the northwest by Daniel O'Sheal.

****

Fussele, Thomas
200 acres in St. George Parish

Granted on October 6, 1767   Grant Book F, page 380

200 acres on Beaver Dam Creek bounded on the southwest by the said Thomas Fussele.

Fussell, Thomas
175 acres in St. George Parish

Granted on December 4, 1770   Grant Book I, page 218

175 acres bounded on the northeast by James Young, northwest
by John Duhart, partly on the southwest by John Duhart and
partly by vacant land and on all other sides by vacant land.

****

Galasper, James
200 acres in St. George Parish

Granted on August 1, 1769   Grant Book G, page 388

200 acres bounded on all sides by vacant land.

****

Galphin, George
100 acres in St. George Parish

Granted on October 29, 1765   Grant Book E, page 284

100 acres bounded on the northwest by McBeans Creek.

****

Galphin, George
1400 acres in St. George Parish

Granted on March 3, 1767   Grant Book F, page 112

1400 acres bounded on the west by the Great Ogechee River.

****

Galphin, George
50 acres in St. George Parish

Granted on April 7, 1767   Grant Book F, page 178

50 acres bounded on the northwest by the Creek of McBeans
Swamp and northeast by the said George Galphin.

****

Galphin, George
300 acres in St. George Parish

Granted on October 4, 1768   Grant Book G, page 195

300 acres bounded on the east by land already laid out and on all other sides by vacant land.

****

Galphin, George
100 acres in St. George Parish

Granted on February 5, 1771   Grant Book I, page 249

100 acres bounded on the southwest by Ogechee River, southeast by land of the said grantee, partly on the northwest by Joseph Marshall and partly by land vacant and on the northeast by land vacant.

****

Galphin, George
100 acres in St. George and St. Paul Parishes

Granted on February 5, 1771   Grant Book I, page 251

100 acres bounded partly on the northeast by land of the said grantee, southeast by Thomas Galphin and on all other sides by vacant land.

****

Galphin, George
150 acres in St. George Parish

Granted on March 3, 1772   Grant Book I, page 528

150 acres bounded on the northwest by Davis.

****

Galphin, George
500 acres in St. George and St. Paul Parishes

Granted on July 7, 1772   Grant Book I, page 655

500 acres bounded on the east by Quintin Pooler.

****

Galphin, George
300 acres in St. George Parish

Granted on January 19, 1773   Grant Book I, page 854

300 acres bounded on all sides by vacant land.

****

Galphin, George
250 acres in St. George Parish

Granted on January 19, 1773   Grant Book I, page 855

250 acres bounded on the northwest by Josham (?) Roberts.

****

Galphin, John
100 acres in St. George Parish

Granted on February 5, 1771   Grant Book I, page 250

100 acres bounded on the southwest by George Galphin.

****

Galphin, Thomas
100 acres in St. George Parish

Granted on March 5, 1771   Grant Book I, page 268

100 acres bounded on all sides by vacant land.

****

Gambell, John
150 acres in St. George Parish

Granted on September 6, 1774   Grant Book M, page 316

150 acres bounded on the northeast by Whitehead.

****

Ganaway, Judith
250 acres in St. George Parish

Granted on January 3, 1775   Grant Book M, page 878

250 acres bounded on the south by Briar Creek, northwest by Margaret Johnson and east by Arthur Wall.

****

Gandy, Samuel
200 acres in St. George Parish

Granted on July 4, 1758   Grant Book A, page 656

200 acres bounded on the west by a branch of Bryar Creek called Rosemary Branch and on all other sides by vacant land.

****

Garvey, James
200 acres in St. George Parish

Granted on May 3, 1768   Grant Book G, page 99

200 acres bounded on the northeast by William Downey.

****

German, George
100 acres in St. George Parish

Surveyed on March 25, 1769   Plat Book C, page 97

100 acres bounded on the east by Benjamin William Bourenon and south by John Gasper Greiner.

****

Germany, James
500 acres in St. George Parish

Granted on July 4, 1758   Grant Book B, page 468

500 acres bounded on the northeast by the Savannah River.

****

Gersham, Joseph
200 acres in St. George Parish

Granted on May 1, 1770   Grant Book I, page 3

200 acres bounded on the southeast and southwest by land of Philip, Kelsall and Monroe and on the northwest by Philip Alston.

****

Gibson, John and Thomas Gibson
250 acres in St. George Parish

Granted on September 6, 1774   Grant Book M, page 313

250 acres bounded on the southeast by William Pendry.

****

Gibson, Samuel
400 acres in St. George Parish

Granted on January 5, 1773   Grant Book I, page 830

400 acres in the Township of Queensborough bounded on the northeast by John Morison and Adam Morison.

****

Gibson, Samuel and William Gibson
200 acres in St. George Parish

Granted on January 6, 1774   Grant Book M, page 312

200 acres in Queensborough and bounded on all sides by vacant land.

****

Gibson, Thomas and John Gibson
250 acres in St. George Parish

Granted on September 6, 1774   Grant Book M, page 313

250 acres bounded on the southeast by William Pendry.

****

Gibson, William and Samuel Gibson
200 acres in St. George Parish

Granted on September 6, 1774   Grant Book M, page 312

200 acres in Queensborough bounded on all sides by vacant land.

****

Gideon, Thomas
200 acres in St. George Parish

Granted January 3, 1769   Grant Book G, page 260

200 acres bounded on all sides by vacant land.

****

Gilmore, John
150 acres in St. George Parish

Original survey date not known
Resurveyed in April 6, 1802   Plat Book M, page 40
Granted on September 6, 1774   Grant Book M, page 319

150 acres in Queensborough bounded on the east by Thomas
Beatty, west by Roger Lawson, northwest by John Allen and
resurveyed in 1802 for Zachariah Lamar.

****

Girvin, Robert
400 acres in St. George Parish

Granted on July 3, 1770   Grant Book I, page 95

Lot 29 in the Town of Queensborough and 400 acres in the
Township of Queensborough bounded on the east by Lamberts
Creek, partly by Joseph Sanders on the west and part by
land vacant on the west, north by William Skelly and on the
south partly by James Habersham and part by Joseph Sanders.

****

Godbe, William
300 acres in St. George Parish

Granted on September 6, 1774   Grant Book M, page 315

300 acres bounded on the southwest by Briar Creek and on the
northwest by Mary Goodall.

****

Godbey, Henry
150 acres in St. George Parish

Granted on April 7, 1767   Grant Book F, page 182

150 acres bounded on all sides by vacant land.

****

Golightly, Charles
200 acres in St. George Parish

Granted on January 1, 1771   Grant Book I, page 236

200 acres bounded on the northeast by James Howell, part
by Elizabeth Bumy and part by land vacant, northwest by
Patrick Brady and on all other sides by land vacant.

****

Goodall, James
211 acres in St. George Parish

Granted on September 1, 1767   Grant Book F, page 348

211 acres bounded on the east by the Savannah River, north
by William McDonald, South by Theobold Keifer and Casper
Rahn.

****

Goodall, Mary
300 acres in St. George Parish

Granted on July 5, 1774   Grant Book M, page 43

300 acres bounded on the northwest by William Moore and on
the southwest by Briar Creek.

****

Goode, John
300 acres in St. George Parish

Granted on September 6, 1768   Grant Book G, page 176

300 acres bounded on all sides by vacant land.

****

Goode, John
250 acres in St. George Parish

Granted on September 6, 1768   Grant Book G, page 177

250 acres bounded on the northeast by Daniel Lott and John
Lott and vacant land, west by Elijah Brasealls and south
by John Goode.

****

Gordon, James
200 acres in St. George Parish

Granted on September 19, 1773   Grant Book I, page 862

200 acres bounded on the west by Joseph Delph.

****

Gordon, John
100 acres in St. George Parish

Granted on May 1, 1759   Grant Book B, page 119

100 acres bounded on the north by Bryer Creek and west by
Richard Schruggs.

****

Gordon, Samuel
150 acres in St. George Parish

Granted on September 6, 1774   Grant Book M, page 320

150 acres in Queensborough Township bounded on the north
by Chavers Creek, east by James Fleming and Edward McConkey,
south by vacant land and west by James Beatty.

****

Graham, John
500 acres in St. George Parish

Granted on February 3, 1767   Grant Book F, page 63

500 acres bounded on all sides by vacant land.

****

Graham, John
500 acres in St. George Parish

Granted on February 3, 1767   Grant Book F, page 64

500 acres bounded on the south partly by land vacant and
partly by Thomas Morgan, northwest partly by land vacant
and partly by William Williams.

****

Graham, John
1000 acres in St. George Parish

Granted on February 3, 1767   Grant Book F, page 65

1000 acres bounded on the southeast by John Howard and on
the northwest by Thomas Morgan.

****

Graham, Thomas
150 acres in St. George Parish

Granted on March 1, 1768   Grant Book G, page 48

150 acres bounded on all sides by vacant land.

****

Graham, Thomas, Robert Rae, John Rae and Samuel Elbert
150 acres in St. George Parish

Granted on November 1, 1774

150 acres bounded on the northeast by Edmund Pearce and
vacant land, southwest by Arthur Wall and west by Isaac
Perry.

****

Graham, Thomas, Robert Rae, James Rae, John Rae, Samuel Elbert
391 acres in St. George Parish

Granted on December 6, 1774   Grant Book M, page 824

391 acres bounded on the northwest by land ordered David
Cavenah, southeast by unknown, northeast by Vacant and
southwest by Great Ogechee River.

****

Graham, Thomas, Robert Rae, James Rae, John Rae, Samuel Elbert
109 acres in St. George Parish

Granted on December 6, 1774   Grant Book M, page 825

109 acres bounded on the east by John Rae, north by ----
Robinson and southwest by Briar Creek.

****

Grant, John
250 acres in St. George Parish

Granted on October 29, 1765   Grant Book E, page 256

250 acres bounded on the northeast by Bryar Creek.

****

Grant, John
100 acres in St. George Parish

Granted on August 4, 1772   Grant Book I, page 704

100 acres bounded on all sides by vacant land.

****

Graves, William
150 acres in St. George Parish

Granted on July 7, 1767   Grant Book F, page 294

150 acres bounded on the north by James Andrew and William
Graves, east by William Quarterman and west by James Andrew.

****

Gray, Catherine
300 acres in St. George Parish

Granted on May 5, 1767   Grant Book F, page 229

300 acres bounded on the southwest by Bryar Creek.

****

Gray, James
100 acres in St. George Parish

Surveyed on October 26, 1759   Plat Book C, page 69
Granted on December 7, 1762   Grant Book D, page 263

Original warrant says, "100 acres in Hallifax District at the head of a place called Toblers (Joblers) Bottom, six miles back of the River Savannah.

****

Gray, James
100 acres in St. George Parish

Granted on February 5, 1765   Grant Book E, page 112

100 acres bounded on the northeast by Savannah River and southeast by Richard Wallis.

****

Gray, James
115 acres in St. George Parish

Granted on January 3, 1775   Grant Book M, page 883

115 acres bounded on the north by Peter Shands, west by the Savannah River and southwest by the said James Gray.

****

Gray, James
200 acres in St. George Parish

Granted on January 3, 1775   Grant Book M, page 884

200 acres bounded on the southeast and northeast by the said James Gray and the Little Beaver Dams.

****

Gray, James
200 acres in St. George Parish

Granted on January 3, 1775   Grant Book M, page 877

200 acres bounded on the southwest by Briar Creek.

****

Gray, James, Jr.
100 acres in St. George Parish

Granted on February 5, 1765   Grant Book E, page 113

100 acres bounded on the northwest by the Savannah River.

****

Gray, Matthias
250 acres in St. George Parish

Granted on May 5, 1767   Grant Book F, page 230

250 acres bounded on all sides by vacant land.

****

Gray, Thomas
100 acres in St. George Parish

Granted on July 7, 1772   Grant Book I, page 662

100 acres bounded on the southwest by Joseph Brantley.

****

Green, John
200 acres in St. George Parish

Granted on February 5, 1771   Grant Book I, page 252

200 acres bounded on all sides by vacant land.

****

Green, William
150 acres in St. George Parish

Surveyed on October 26, 1758   Plat Book C, page 68

Original warrant says, "150 acres in the fork of Briar
Creek about two miles from the mouth of it.

****

Greene, David
200 acres in St. George Parish

Original survey date unknown
Resurveyed on May 22, 1838   Plat Book M, page 130
Granted on September 1, 1767   Grant Book F, page 344

200 acres bounded on the east by Catherine Gray. Resurveyed for William B. Greene and found to contain 347 acres.

****

Greer, David
100 acres in St. George Parish

Granted on July 3, 1770

100 acres in the Township of Queensborough bounded on the east by Rudy Branch, Matthew Moore and James McClavey and south by Thomas Beatty, and also town lot 52 in Queensborough.

****

Greiner, Andrew
200 acres in St. George Parish

Granted on December 3, 1760   Grant Book C, page 306

200 acres bounded on the east by the Savannah River and on the south by John Gasper Herseman.

****

Greiner, Andrew
50 acres in St. George Parish

Surveyed on February 16, 1761   Plat Book C, page 68
Granted on November 27, 1761   Grant Book C, page 347

50 acres bounded on the northeast by Benjamin Williamson and on every other part by the Savannah River. Original warrant says, "on King Creek Island in the Savannah River opposite the Geiner (sic) settlement on the main.

****

Greiner, Andrew
200 acres in St. George Parish

Granted on April 7, 1767   Grant Book F, page 183

200 acres bounded on the north by the Savannah River, east by Thomas Bell, west by William Mainer and south by land of Andrew Greiner and Samuel Royal.

****

Greiner, Andrew
500 acres in St. George Parish

Granted on April 7, 1767   Grant Book F, page 184

500 acres bounded on the east by Samuel Royal, southeast by Samuel Haynes and north by the said Andrew Greiner.

****

Greiner, Catherine M.
500 acres in St. George Parish

Granted on April 13, 1761   Grant Book C, page 140

500 acres bounded on the north by Theobold Keifer, east by the Savannah River and south by Benjamin William Borneman.

****

Greiner, John Gasper
200 acres in St. George Parish

Granted on May 21, 1762   Grant Book D, page 113

200 acres bounded on the east by the Savannah River, north by William McDonald and south by Phillip Jacob Greiner.

****

Greiner, John Martin
250 acres in St. George Parish

Granted on June 7, 1768   Grant Book G, page 121

250 acres bounded on the east by George Streigler and Michael Beaner, southeast by Nicholas Fisher and northeast by John Tanner.

****

Greiner, Phillip Jacob
300 acres in St. George Parish

Granted on April 13, 1761   Grant Book C, page 138

300 acres bounded on the north by Jacob Hensler and east by
the Savannah River.

****

Greiner, Philip Jacob
150 acres in St. George Parish

Granted on April 7, 1767   Grant Book F, page 185

150 acres bounded on the south by a Great Lake lying between
the said tract and land of John Royal, east by the Savannah
River, north and west by Thomas Bell, James Gray and
Richard Wallace.

****

Gretion, John
100 acres in St. George Parish

Granted on September 6, 1774   Grant Book M, page 318

100 acres bounded on the northeast by Briar Creek, southwest by John Gretion and land surveyed for Mr. McKay.

****

Griener, John Gasper
100 acres in St. George Parish

Granted on May 1, 1764   Grant Book E, page 8

100 acres bounded on the west by Briar Creek.

****

Grienier, Peter
450 acres in St. George and St. Matthew Parishes

Granted on January 5, 1768   Grant Book E, page 5

450 acres bounded on all sides by vacant land.

****

Griner, John Gasper
1000 acres in St. George Parish

Granted on August 2, 1774   Grant Book M, page 191

1000 acres bounded on the north by William Boseman, east
by Jacob Griner, John Dunn, William Web and Glebe Land.

****

Groves, Allen
300 acres in St. George Parish

Granted on April 7, 1772   Grant Book I, page 555

300 acres bounded on the east by John Mann and John Grant,
north by Briar Creek and west by Edward Barnard.

****

Guin, Roan
200 acres in St. George Parish

Granted on July 2, 1771   Grant Book I, page 362

200 acres bounded on the northeast by Moodie's land.

****

Habersham, James
500 acres in St. George Parish

Granted on June 7, 1774   Grant Book I, page 1058

500 acres bounded on the northwest by James Habersham.

****

Habersham, James
800 acres in St. George Parish

Granted on June 7, 1774   Grant Book I, page 1075

800 acres bounded partly on the southwest by ---Finley and
on all other sides by vacant land.

****

Habersham, James
500 acres in St. George Parish

Granted on June 7, 1774   Grant Book I, page 1079

500 acres bounded on the southeast by the said James Habersham.

****

Hadin, James
250 acres in St. George Parish

Granted on July 3, 1770   Grant Book I, page 97

250 acres in the Township of Queensborough bounded on the
south by William McCay and Matthew Moore, west by Joseph
Sanders, north by Joseph Girvin and east by Lambeth's
Creek, and also town lot 8 in the Town of Queensborough.

****

Hadon, William
100 acres in St. George Parish

Granted on September 6, 1774   Grant Book M, page 322

100 acres in Queensborough Township bounded on the east by
Lamberts Creek, west by McCalvey, north by Andrew Humbleton
and south by Cloty Robson and also town lot 27 in the
Town of Queensborough.

****

Hamilton, Andrew
100 acres in St. George Parish

Granted on August 2, 1774   Grant Book M, page 206

100 acres in Queensborough bounded on the east by------
Crossly, west by Matthew Moore, north by James Haddin
and south by land surveyed for Patrick McKay.

****

Hamilton, Jean and John Hamilton and Mary Ledger
500 acres in St. George Parish

Granted on May 2, 1775   Grant Book M, page 1115

500 acres in Queensborough and bounded on the northwest by David Munrow.

****

Hamilton, John and Mary Ledger and Jean Hamilton
500 acres in St. George Parish

Granted on May 2, 1775   Grant Book M, page 1115

500 acres in Queensborough and bounded on the northwest
by David Munrow.

****

Hamilton, Robert
250 acres in St. George Parish

Granted on March 7, 1775   Grant Book M, page 1075

250 acres bounded on the east by Thomas Lowers.

****

Hamilton, Thomas
200 acres in St. George Parish

Original survey date unknown
Resurveyed on February 16, 1836   Plat Book M, page 129
Granted on November 1, 1774   Grant Book M, page 670

200 acres resurveyed for John H. Cox and found to contain
225 acres.

****

Hammond, William
100 acres in St. George Parish

Granted on October 3, 1769   Grant Book G, page 434

100 acres bounded on all sides by vacant land.

****

Hammond, William
150 acres in St. George Parish

Granted on February 7, 1775   Grant Book M, page 1003

150 acres bounded on the northeast by William Hammond and on the southwest by William Alexander.

****

Hampton, John
100 acres in St. George Parish

Granted on August 2, 1774   Grant Book M, page 204

100 acres bounded on the northeast by Asa Emanuel, south by Hall Hudson, southeast by David Lewis and west by John Nelson.

****

Handley, William
300 acres in St. George Parish

Granted on August 2, 1763   Grant Book D, page 314

300 acres bounded on the northeast, northwest and southeast by the said William Handley and southwest by John Burnsides.

****

Handley, William
100 acres in St. George Parish

Granted on August 2, 1763   Grant Book D, page 315

100 acres bounded on the northwest by the said William Handley and on the southwest by Thomas Cawdry.

****

Handley, William
500 acres in St. George Parish

Granted on July 5, 1774   Grant Book M, page 98

500 acres granted to James Read and James Deveaux in trust for William Handley and bounded on the northwest by Nunes and John Lott.

****

William Handley
500 acres in St. George Parish

Original survey date unknown
Resurveyed on May 19, 1829   Plat Book M, page 124
Granted on July 5, 1774   Grant Book M, page 97

500 acres bounded on the south by ----Pray, west by Helvenstine and east by Bledsoe. Resurveyed in 1829 for Joshua
Clebbon and found to contain 378 acres.

****

Harding, William
100 acres in St. George Parish

Granted on July 3, 1770   Grant Book I, page 96

100 acres in the Township of Queensborough bounded on the
southeast by the Great Ogechee River, northeast by Lambeths
Big Creek, partly on the northwest by Clotworthy Robson
and part by town lots and southwest by the Town Common,
and also Town Lot 56 in the Town of Queensborough.

****

Harding, William
200 acres in St. George Parish

Granted on November 1, 1774   Grant Book M, page 673

200 acres bounded on the southwest by Ogechee River and
Lamberts Creek, north by Parkinson, east by Samuel
Tomlinson and Harden and south by Pooler.

****

Hare, Benjamin
100 acres in St. George Parish

Granted on August 2, 1774   Grant Book M, page 196

100 acres bounded on the northeast by Briar Creek.

****

Harnage, George
100 acres in St. George Parish

Granted on October 29, 1765   Grant Book E, page 313

100 acres bounded on all sides by vacant land.

Harnage, George
100 acres in St. George Parish

Granted on September 1, 1767   Grant Book F, page 350

100 acres bounded on all sides by vacant land.

****

Harnage, Jacob
200 acres in St. George Parish

Granted on April 7, 1772   Grant Book I, page 559

200 acres bounded on the north by Beaver Dam Creek.

****

Harragan, Patrick

300 acres in St. George Parish

Granted on November 7, 1769   Grant Book G, page 460

300 acres bounded on the southwest by Edward Pilsher, southeast by vacant land and the said William Pilsher and northeast by William Davis and vacant land.

****

Harris, James
300 acres in St. George Parish

Granted on September 6, 1774   Grant Book M, page 331

300 acres bounded on the east by Henry Sharp.

****

Harrison, Thomas
250 acres in St. George Parish

Granted on February 7, 1775   Grant Book M, page 1005

250 acres bounded on the south by Benjamin Lewis, northeast by John Sharp, north by Hall Hudson and west by David Lewis.

****

Harvey, John
150 acres in St. George Parish

Granted on October 2, 1770   Grant Book I, page 173

150 acres bounded on all sides by vacant land.

****

Hawthorn, Robert
200 acres in St. George Parish

Granted on June 7, 1774   Grant Book I, page 1073

200 acres bounded on the southwest by Elizabeth Burney and
on all other sides by vacant land.

****

Hayman, Henry
200 acres in St. George Parish

Granted on September 6, 1774   Grant Book M, page 325

200 acres bounded on all sides by vacant land.

****

Haynes, Samuel
200 acres in St. George Parish

Surveyed on February 18, 1761   Plat Book C, page 78
Granted on April 2, 1765   Grant Book E, page 128

200 acres bounded on the southeast by John Royal. The plat
of survey shows that the land is located on Great Sweetwater
Creek with Kings Road running through it.

****

Headrick, Alexander
100 acres in St. George Parish

Granted on May 4, 1773   Grant Book I, page 977

100 acres bounded on the northwest by Thomas Russell and on
the southwest by James Read

****

Headrick, Alexander
150 acres in St. George Parish

Granted on November 1, 1774   Grant Book M, page 669

150 acres bounded on the southwest by the said Alexander
Headrick and Thomas Fussell and on the northwest by
Thomas Fussell and vacant land.

****

Heaton, Isaac
200 acres in St. George Parish

Granted on October 3, 1769   Grant Book G, page 435

200 acres bounded on all sides by vacant land.

****

Heaton, Richard
200 acres in St. George Parish

Granted on July 2, 1765   Grant Book E, page 175

200 acres bounded on the north by the Savannah River and
on the east by Benjamin Goldwire.

****

Heaton, Robert
300 acres in St. George Parish

Granted on October 2, 1764   Grant Book E, page 42

300 acres located about three miles above the mouth of
Buckhead Creek and about two miles below land settled by
John Davies and bounded on all sides by vacant land.

****

Heekle, William
300 acres in St. George Parish

Granted on August 2, 1774   Granted Book M, page 197

300 acres bounded on the northeast by William Lord.

****

Heislear, George
250 acres in St. George Parish

Granted March 1, 1768   Grant Book G, page 49

250 acres bounded on all sides by vacant land.

****

Henderson, John
400 acres in St. George Parish

Surveyed on November 17, 1771   Plat Book M, page 113
Granted on May 5, 1772   Grant Book I, page 593

400 acres bounded on the southeast by Frederick Francis and
William Newberry.

****

Hendrick, Hans
300 acres in St. George Parish

Granted on June 2, 1767   Grant Book F, page 269

300 acres bounded on the north by Thomas Burrington and on
all other sides by vacant land.

****

Herbert, James
200 acres in St. George Parish

Granted on November 1, 1774   Grant Book M, page 671

200 acres bounded on the northeast by Briar Creek, southwest
by the said James Herbert, southeast by Allan Groves and
northwest by William Sapp.

****

Hersham, John Gasper
300 acres in St. George Parish

Granted on November 1, 1774   Grant Book M, page 672

300 acres bounded on the east by Abraham Lundy and Mordecai
Sheftall and north by the said John Gasper Hersham.

****

87A

Hescut, William
100 acres in St. George Parish

Granted on September 6, 1774   Grant Book M, page 323

100 acres bounded on all sides by vacant land.

****

Hickey, Mary
50 acres in St. George Parish

Granted on May 4, 1773   Grant Book H, page 100

50 acres on bounty bounded partly on the north by McBeans
Creek, east by Zachariah Fam and on all other sides by
vacant land at the time of the survey.

****

Hill, Edmund
150 acres in St. George Parish

Granted on February 7, 1775   Grant Book M, page 1007

150 acres bounded on the southwest and the northwest by
William Brown.

****

Hirshman, John Jasper, Jr.
250 acres in St. George Parish

Granted on April 13, 1761   Grant Book C, page 136

250 acres bounded on the north by /illegible/, east by the
Savannah River and south by Michael Zeigler.

****

Hobbs, William
150 acres in St. George Parish

Granted on March 3, 1772   Grant Book I, page 530

150 acres bounded on the southeast by David Russell, northeast by Richard Scruggs and James Houston.

****

Hogg, James
150 acres in St. George Parish

Granted on December 6, 1774   Grant Book M, page 797

150 acres bounded on the northwest by John Grant.

****

Hollingsworth, Valentine
50 acres in St. George Parish

Granted on July 5, 1774   Grant Book H, page 107

50 acres bounded on the southeast by land of the said
Valentine Hollingsworth.

****

Hollingsworth, Valentine
200 acres in St. George Parish

Granted on January 7, 1772   Grant Book I, page 495

200 acres bounded on all sides by vacant land.

****

Hollingsworth, Valentine
150 acres in St. George Parish

Surveyed on November 25, 1771   Plat Book M, page 49
Granted on October 6, 1772   Grant Book I, page 780

150 acres bounded on the east by John Mann, west by Abraham
Sapp and south by Stephen Murray.

****

Hollingsworth, Zebulon
150 acres in St. George Parish

Granted on August 2, 1774   Grant Book M, page 201

150 acres bounded on all sides by vacant land.

****

Holmes, David
150 acres in St. George Parish

Granted on April 6, 1773   Grant Book I, page 950

150 acres bounded on the south by land of Helvenstine. (?).

****

Holmes, David
150 acres in St. George Parish

Grant on March 1, 1768   Grant Book G, page 50

150 acres bounded on the west by Lamberts Big Creek.

****

Holmes, David
100 acres in St. George Parish

Granted on June 5, 1771   Grant Book I, page 342

100 acres bounded on all sides by vacant land.

****

Hooker, Nathan
100 acres in St. George Parish

G_ranted on May 7, 1765   Grant Book E, page 152

100 acres bounded on all sides by vacant land.

****

Hooker, Nathan
100 acres in St. George Parish

Granted on December 2, 1766   Grant Book F, page 3

100 acres bounded on the southeast by Nathan Hooker.

****

Hopkins, John
150 acres in St. George Parish

Surveyed on November 29, 1759   Plat Book C, page 78
Granted on July 7, 1761   Grant Book D, page 57

150 acres bounded on the east by the Savannah River.

****

Horn, Benjamin
200 acres in St. George Parish

Granted on December 3, 1760   Grant Book C, page 27

200 acres bounded on the north by the Savannah River and west by John Sisson.

****

Horn, Benjamin
100 acres in St. George Parish

Granted on February 2, 1768   Grant Book G, page 23

100 acres bounded on all sides by vacant land.

****

Horton, Nicholas
500 acres in St. George Parish

Granted on November 3, 1767   Grant Book F, page 406

500 acres bounded on the northeast by Bryar Creek, northwest by Sarah Bevil and southeast by William Colston.

****

Houlton, Samuel
150 acres in St. George Parish

Granted on December 4, 1770   Grant Book I, page 220

150 acres bounded on all sides by vacant land.

****

Houston, John
500 acres in St. George Parish

Granted on October 4, 1774   Grant Book M, page 455

500 acres bounded on the southwest by Philip Minis and southwest by Buckhead Creek.

****

Houston, John and George Baillie
1000 acres in St. George Parish

Granted on August 2, 1774   Grant Book M, page 208

1000 acres bounded on the southeast by Thomas Lewis, southwest by Walker and Thomas Yarbrough.

****

Houston, Sir Patrick
100 acres in St. George Parish

Granted on October 6, 1772   Grant Book I, page 769

100 acres bounded on the east by William O'Bryan and on the
north by Philip Dell.

****

Howart, John
100 acres in St. George Parish

Granted on October 29, 1765   Grant Book E, page 257

100 acres bounded on the west by Briar Creek and on the south
by Solomon Kemp.

****

Howell, David
150 acres in St. George Parish

Original survey date unknown
Resurveyed on August 18, 1824   Plat Book M, page 111
Granted on September 1, 1767   Granted book F, page 349

150 acres bounded on the northwest by John Howell, on the
southwest by John Rae and on the southeast by Andrew Lambert.
Resurveyed for William Green and Harley Attaway in 1824 and
found to contain 175 acres.

****

Howell, David
100 acres in St. George Parish

Granted on July 7, 1772   Grant Book I, page 677

100 acres bounded on the south by James Douglass and west
by the land of the said grantee.

                         ****

Howell, James
100 acres in St. George Parish

Granted on March 3, 1767   Grant Book F, page 114

100 acres on Buckhead Creek and bounded on the east by
Elizabeth Burney, widow.

                         ****

Howell, John
100 acres in St. George Parish

Granted October 29, 1765   Grant Book E, page 310

100 acres bounded on the northwest by Charles Gee.

                         ****

Howell, John, Jr.
150 acres in St. George Parish

Granted August 2, 1968   Grant Book G, page 152

150 acres bounded on the southwest by John Howell and on
the west by Charles Gee.

                         ****

Hubbard, Richard
200 acres in St. George Parish

Granted on September 25, 1760   Grant Book B, page 430

200 acres bounded on the southeast by vacant land and on every
other side by the Savannah River and King Creek.

                         ****

Hubbard, Richard
100 acres in St. George Parish

Granted on September 25, 1760   Grant Book B, page 431

100 acres bounded on the east by the Savannah River, south
by Andrew Griner and north by Andrew McCurrie.

****

Hudson, Hale
200 acres in St. George Parish

Granted on November 3, 1767   Grant Book F, page 405

200 acres bounded on the southwest by David Lewis and on
the southeast by David Emanuel.

****

Hudson, Hall
100 acres in St. George Parish

Granted on July 5, 1774   Grant Book M, page 46

100 acres bounded on the southeast by David Emanuel, northeast by William Case and southwest by the said Hall Hudson.

****

Hudson, Robert
100 acres in St. George Parish

Granted on February 7, 1758   Grant Book B, page 32

100 acres in the District of Halifax bounded on the east
by the Savannah River.

****

Hudson, Robert
150 acres in St. George Parish

Surveyed on October 21, 1758   Plat Book C, page 78
Granted on May 1, 1759   Grant Book B, page 507

150 acres bounded on the south by Anthony Thomas, west by
Southerland and east by Samuel Jordan.

****

Hudson, Samuel
400 acres in St. George Parish

Granted on February 7, 1758   Grant Book B, page 539

400 acres in the District of Halifax bounded on the east by
the Savannah River.

****

Hudson, Samuel
100 acres in St. George Parish

Granted on April 3, 1764   Grant Book D, page 408

100 acres bounded on the east by the Savannah River, north by
John Brady and south by Samuel Hudson.

****

Hume, James
1000 acres in St. George Parish

Granted on September 3, 1771   Grant Book I, page 407

1000 acres bounded partly on the northwest by land surveyed
for John Powell, southwest by the Great Ogechee River and
on all other sides by vacant land.

****

Humphries, Joseph
100 acres in St. George Parish

Granted on April 6, 1773   Grant Book I, page 948

100 acres bounded on the north by Anderson and on the east
by Morgan.

****

Humphreys, Joseph
250 acres in St. George Parish

Granted on September 6, 1768   Grant Book G, page 178

250 acres bounded on the south by Briar Creek.

****

Humphreys, Robert
250 acres in St. George Parish

Granted on December 6, 1763   Grant Book D, page 361

250 acres bounded on the northeast by the Savannah River and on the northwest by William Handley.

****

Huston, James
400 acres in St. George Parish

Granted on May 1, 1759   Grant Book B, page 127

400 acres in the District of Halifax bounded on all sides by vacant land.

****

Ingram, John
400 acres in St. George Parish

Surveyed on May 15, 1770   Plat Book C, page 101
Granted on August 2, 1774   Grant Book M, page 209

400 acres in Queensborough bounded on the northeast by William McLeroy and vacant land, northwest by Walter Stevens and vacant land, southeast by Jacob Winfree and Robert Cooper and south by Robert Cooper.

****

Irbey, Henry
400 acres in St. George Parish

Surveyed on March 27, 1770   Plat Book C, page 100
Granted on October 1, 1771   Grant Book I, page 431

400 acres bounded on the south by Dukes Pond.

****

Irvin, David
150 acres in St. George Parish

Surveyed on December 23, 1772   Plat Book C, page 100
Granted on September 6, 1774   Grant Book M, page 332

150 acres bounded on the southeast by Jared Irwin and also surveyed as Irwin.

****

Irvin, Isabell
300 acres in St. George Parish

Surveyed on March 17, 1773   Plat Book C, page 102
Granted on August 2, 1774   Grant Book M, page 210

300 acres in Queensborough and bounded on the north by Edward Seaburn and John Fulton and south by James Hamilton.

****

Irvin, Isabell
150 acres in St. George Parish

Surveyed on July 22, 1772   Plat Book C, page 100
Granted on August 2, 1774   Grant Book M, page 211

150 acres in Queensborough and bounded on the northwest by Robert Breison.

****

Irwin, Jared
150 acres in St. George Parish

Surveyed on October 24, 1768   Plat Book C, page 98
Granted on March 7, 1769   Grant Book G, page 279

150 acres bounded on all sides by vacant land.

****

Irwin, Thomas
250 acres in St. George Parish

Surveyed on May 19, 1758   Plat Book C, page 96
Granted on January 5, 1762   Grant Book D, page 8

Original warrant states that the tract was located on the south side of Walnut Branch, running into Briar Creek where Thomas Irwin is already settled.

****

Irwin, Thomas
100 acres in St. George Parish

Surveyed on May 14, 1760   Plat Book C, page 97
Granted on January 5, 1762   Grant Book D, page 9

100 acres bounded on the northeast by the said Thomas Irwin,
southeast by Peter Elliott and northwest by David Emanuel.
Original warrant states that the tract joined on the west
by lands formerly granted to Thomas Irwin in Halifax District.

****

Irwin, Thomas
300 acres in St. George Parish

Granted on May 7, 1765   Grant Book E, page 139

300 acres bounded on the west by James Huston and north by
Bryar Creek.

****

Irwin, Thomas
150 acres in St. George Parish

Surveyed on June 23, 1767   Plat Book C, page 98
Granted on January 5, 1768   Grant Book G, page 9

150 acres bounded on all sides by vacant land.

****

Irwin, Thomas
350 acres in St. George Parish

Surveyed on November 13, 1762   Plat Book C, page 338

350 acres bounded on the north and east by the Savannah River,
north by Nehemiah Tindall and south by Robert Bevil. Original
warrant states that this was surveyed for Richard Scruggs,
thence ordered to Thomas Irwin on October 2, 1764.

****

Jarman, George
100 acres in St. George Parish

Granted on August 1, 1769   Grant Book G, page 389

100 acres bounded on the south by John Casper Griener and on the east by Benjamin William Borneman.

****

Jenkin, William
100 acres in St. George Parish

Granted on October 4, 1774   Grant Book M, page 564

100 acres in Queensborough bounded on the southeast by land supposed to belong to James Haddon, northeast by John Wilson and northwest by John McNeely.

****

Jenkins, Francis
250 acres in St. George Parish

Granted on November 4, 1766   Grant Book E, page 391

250 acres bounded on all sides by vacant land.

****

Jenkins, Francis
400 acres in St. George Parish

Granted on October 6, 1767   Grant Book F, page 381

400 acres bounded on the northwest by Henry Baker.

****

Jenkins, Owens
250 acres in St. George Parish

Granted on July 7, 1767   Grant Book F, page 298

250 acres bounded on all sides by vacant land.

****

Jernigan, Ann
150 acres in St. George Parish

Surveyed on June 15, 1768   Plat Book C, page 99
Granted on January 3, 1775   Grant Book M, page 893

150 acres bounded on the north by Buckhead Creek, south and west by John Moore and John Warnack and surveyed as Ann Jarnigan.

****

John, David
100 acres in St. George Parish

Surveyed on March 12, 1759   Plat Book C, page 96
Granted on April 2, 1765   Grant Book E, page 157

100 acres bounded on the northeast by David Lewis. The original warrant states that the tract was located in the fork of Brier Creek about 1 mile from the land of William Champ.

****

John, Moore, widow
150 acres in St. George Parish

Granted on May 5, 1767   Grant Book F, page 235

150 acres bounded on all sides by vacant land.

****

Johnson, Lewis
1500 acres in St. George and St. Matthew Parish

Granted on July 7, 1767   Grant Book F, page 297

1500 acres partly in the tow parishes and bounded on the west by land laid out for Alexander Wylly, east partly by Bryan Kelly and partly by land vacant.

****

Johnson, Margaret
300 acres in St. George Parish

Surveyed on November 20, 1766   Plat Book C, page 99
Granted on September 6, 1768   Grant Book G, page 179

300 acres bounded on the northwest by Absalom Wells, south by Briar Creek and surveyed as Margaret Johnston.

****

Johnston, William
200 acres in St. George Parish

Surveyed on January 22, 1768   Plat Book C, page 97
Granted on April 5, 1768   Grant Book G, page 75

200 acres in vacant land.

****

Jones, Edward
300 acres in St. George Parish

Granted on March 7, 1775   Grant Book M, page 1077

300 acres bounded on the northwest by William Moxley and
on the southwest by Patrick Brady.

****

Jones, Henry
350 acres in St. George Parish

Granted on January 3, 1775   Grant Book M, page 888

350 acres bounded on the south by Buckhead Creek and Josias
Dickson, north by vacant land and on the northeast by
Thomas and George Wyche.

****

Jones, James
150 acres in St. George Parish

Surveyed on July 30, 1766   Plat Book C, page 98
Granted on June 7, 1768   Grant Book G, page 123

150 acres bounded on the south by Briar Creek, southeast by
land ordered Isaac Copeland and on the northwest by Solomon
Kemp.

****

Jones, Noble Wimberly
1800 acres in St. George Parish

Surveyed on August 26, 1770   Plat Book C, page 101
Granted on January 1, 1771   Grant Book I, page 238

1800 acres bounded on all sides by vacant land.

****

Jones, Richard
250 acres in St. George Parish

Surveyed on November 25, 1765   Plat Book C, page 97

250 acres bounded on all sides by vacant land.

****

Jones, Thomas

See Elphinson, Philip at page 55 of this volume.

****

Jordan, James
200 acres in St. George Parish

Surveyed on Janaury 27, 1770   Plat Book C, page 99

200 acres bounded on the west by James Anderson and Joseph
Delap.

****

Jordan, Matthew
150 acres in St. George Parish

Surveyed on November 20, 1769   Plat Book C, page 99
Granted on February 4, 1772   Grant Book I, page 510

150 acres bounded on the northeast by James Anderson, deceased.

****

Jordan, William
400 acres in St. George Parish

Surveyed on March 1, 1769   Plat Book C, page 98
Granted on May 2, 1769   Grant Book G, page 316

400 acres bounded on the west by James Anderson.

****

Jordan, William, Jr.
450 acres in St. George Parish

Granted on January 3, 1775   Grant Book M, page 892

450 acres bounded on the east by Wyche and Delap.

****

Kamp, Jonathon
100 acres in St. George Parish

Surveyed on December 17, 1770   Plat Book C, page 121
Granted on September 3, 1771   Grant Book I, page 417

100 acres bounded on the northwest by William Underwood.

****

Keebler, John
450 acres in St. George Parish

Surveyed on July 18, 1771   Plat Book C, page 123
                                   Plat Book M, page 127
Granted on December 3, 1771   Grant Book I, page 479

450 acres resurveyed on November 19, 1827 for Wright Murphrey
and found to contain 500 acres.

****

Kelly, David
100 acres in St. George Parish

Surveyed on December 4, 1772   Plat Book C, page 121
Granted on September 6, 1774   Grant Book M, page 337

100 acres bounded on the southeast by----Sheftall and on the
northwest by William Lord.

****

Kelsall, Roger and Simon Munro
1000 acres in St. George Parish

Surveyed on September 25, 1766   Plat Book C, page 121
Granted on February 2, 1768   Grant Book G, page 24

1000 acres bounded on the northeast partly by Philip Alston and partly by John Waters. Plat shows Alexander Lamar also on the northeast.

****

Kelsall, Roger and Simon Munro
100 acres in St. George Parish

Surveyed on September 24, 1766   Plat Book C, page 121
Granted on February 2, 1768   Grant Book G, page 26

100 acres bounded on the north by the Savannah River.

****

Kelsall, Roger and Simon Munro
200 acres in St. George Parish

Surveyed on October 27, 1766   Plat Book C, page 121
Granted on March 1, 1768   Grant Book G, page 51

200 acres bounded on the north by Zachariah Fenn, northeast by Philip Alston and southeast by Alexander Lamar.

****

Kelsall, Roger and Simon Munro
100 acres in St. George Parish

Granted on March 1, 1768   Grant Book G, page 52

100 acres bounded by Zachariah Fenn and Alexander Lamar.

****

Kemp, Solomon
100 acres in St. George Parish

Granted on October 2, 1764   Grant Book E, page 46

100 acres bounded on the south by Bryar Creek.

****

Kemp, Solomon
100 acres in St. George Parish

Granted on September 2, 1774   Grant Book M, page 339

100 acres bounded on the southeast by James Jones, northeast
by Briar Creek and northwest by the said Solomon Kemp.

****

Kennedy, Daniel
350 acres in St. George Parish

Surveyed on September 6, 1761   Plat Book C, page 120

350 acres bounded on the northeast by the Savannah River,
northwest by Darby Canadey. Original warrant states that
the tract was in Halifax District at Stony Bluff on the
River Savannah adjoining land heretofore granted him and
land of Derby Kennedy.

****

Kennedy, Darby
100 acres in St. George Parish
Granted on September 4, 1764   Grant Book E, page 29

100 acres located at the ferry over Briar Creek and bounded
on the northeast by Briar Creek.

****

Kennedy, Darby
350 acres in St. George Parish

Granted on September 4, 1764   Grant Book E, page 31

350 acres bounded on the northeast by the Savannah River and
on the northwest by the said Darby Kennedy.

****

Kennedy, Darby
100 acres in St. George Parish

Surveyed on April 3, 1756   Plat Book C, page 130
Granted on August 7, 1764   Grant Book E, page 25

100 acres bounded on east by Savannah River and surveyed as
Darby Kennedy in Halifax District. Original warrant states
that the tract was located at a place known by the name of
Stony Bluff about 6 miles above Mr. Borreman's plantation
at Hallifax, bounded on all sides by vacant land.

****

Kennedy, John
100 acres in St. George Parish

Surveyed on May 17, 1758   Plat Book C, page 117
Granted on September 4, 1764   Grant Book E, page 33

100 acres bounded on the northeast by the Savannah River,
southeast by Darby Kennedy and surveyed as in St. Paul
Parish. Original warrant states that the tract is located
on the upper side of Stony Bluff near Hallifax.

****

Kennedy, John
250 acres in St. George Parish

Surveyed on June 12, 1769   Plat Book C, page 121
Granted on July 3, 1770   Grant Book I, page 98

250 acres in the Township of Queensborough and also lot 7
in the Town of Queensborough bounded on the northwest by
Black Jack Branch.

****

Kettle, Jacob
100 acres in St. George Parish

Granted on October 29, 1765   Grant Book E, page 300
100 acres bounded on the northeast by John Warnok.

****

Kincaid, George
600 acres in St. George Parish

Surveyed on December 3, 1771   Plat Book C, page 123
Granted on January 7, 1772   Grant Book I, page 497

600 acres bounded on all sides by vacant land.

****

Kincaid, George
600 acres in St. George Parish

Surveyed on November 28, 1771   Plat Book C, page 123
Granted on April 7, 1772   Grant Book I, page 563

600 acres bounded on all sides by vacant land.

Kincaid, George
600 acres in St. George Parish

Surveyed on December 6, 1771   Plat Book C, page 124
Granted on June 2, 1772   Grant Book I, page 633

600 acres bounded on the north by ---Baillie.

****

Kitt, John
350 acres in St. George Parish

Surveyed on June 12, 1758   Plat Book C, page 121
Granted on February 5, 1760   Grant Book C, page 176

350 acres bounded on the northeast by Savannah River and
northwest by William Lindall.

****

Knobelock, John
100 acres in St. George Parish

Surveyed on December 8, 1767   Plat Book C, page 121
Granted on July 5, 1768   Grant Book G, page 137

100 acres bounded on all sides by vacant land.

****

LaMar, William
300 acres in St. George Parish

Granted on May 1, 1764   Grant Book E, page 12

300 acres bounded on the northeast by the Savannah River
and on the southeast by Daniel Wallicon.

****

Lamar, Zachariah

See John Gilmore at page 70 of this volume.

****

Lamb, Abraham
200 acres in St. George Parish

Granted on September 1, 1767   Grant Book F, page 352

200 acres bounded on all sides by vacant land.

****

Lamb, Abraham
200 acres in St. George Parish

Surveyed on December 4, 1767   Plat Book C, page 140
Granted on April 3, 1770   Grant Book G, page 578

200 acres bounded on the north by the said Abraham Lamb.

****

Lamb, Thomas
150 acres in St. George Parish

Granted on August 4, 1767   Grant Book F, page 319

150 acres bounded on the southeast by John Rae and John Kennedy,
and on every other side by land vacant at the time of the
survey which said tract was heretofore ordered Benjamin Moore.

****

Lamb, Thomas
100 acres in St. George Parish

Granted on March 1, 1768   Grant Book G, page 53

100 acres bounded on all sides by vacant land.

****

Lambert, Andrew
200 acres in St. George Parish

Surveyed on October 16, 1765   Plat Book C, page 142
Granted on June 7, 1768   Grant Book G, page 127

200 acre tract surveyed for Andrew Lambert, then ordered to
Mordecai and Levi Sheftall and granted to them.

****

Lambert, Andrew
400 acres in St. George Parish

Surveyed on October 16, 1765   Plat Book C, page 142
Granted on June 7, 1768   Grant Book G, page 126

400 acre tract surveyed for Andrew Lambert, thence ordered
on February 2, 1768, to Mordecai and Levi Sheftall. Granted
to Mordecai and Levi Sheftall.

****

Lambert, James
200 acres in St. George Parish

Granted on January 5, 1768   Grant Book G, page 11

200 acres bounded on all sides by vacant land.

****

Lambert, James
200 acres in St. George Parish

Granted on July 4, 1769   Grant Book G, page 359

200 acres bounded on the southwest by the Great Ogechee
River and on the east and north by the said James Lambert.

****

Lambert, James
50 acres in St. George Parish

Surveyed on August 20, 1771   Plat Book C, page 144
Granted on November 5, 1771   Grant Book H, page 62

50 acres bounded on the east by James Lambert, north by
Anthony Stokes and south by John Womack.

****

Lambert, James
50 acres in St. George Parish

Surveyed on May 12, 1772   Plat Book C, page 144

50 acres bounded on all sides by vacant land.

****

Lanier, Lemuel
200 acres in St. George Parish

Surveyed on June 1, 1770   Plat Book C, page 338
Granted on August 6, 1771   Grant Book I, page 385

200 acres bounded on the northeast by the Savannah River,
southeast by John Frazer, north by Peter Torquintz, northwest
by vacant land and partly on the southwest by Mordecai
Sheftall and part by land vacant. Originally surveyed for
Francis Stringer, then ordered to Lemuel Lanier on June 5, 1771.

****

Larecy, Mary, widow of John Larecy, deceased
100 acres in St. George Parish

Granted on July 2, 1765   Grant Book E, page 174

100 acres located on the south side of Bryar Creek.

****

Large, John
300 acres in St. George Parish

Surveyed on January 6, 1768   Plat Book C, page 141
Granted on September 6, 1768   Grant Book G, page 181

300 acres bounded on all sides by vacant land.

****

Larimore, Isaac
200 acres in St. George Parish

Granted on December 6, 1774   Grant Book M, page 802

200 acres bounded on the north by James Simpson and south by
William Mosley.

****

Lawson, Roger
300 acres in St. George Parish

Granted on September 6, 1763   Grant Book D, page 326

300 acres on south side of Bryar Creek and north by Richard Sarogs.

****

Lawson, Roger
200 acres in St. George Parish

Granted on March 3, 1767   Grant Book F, page 128

200 acres bounded on all sides by vacant land.

****

Lawson, Roger
150 acres in St. George Parish

Surveyed on November 21, 1769   Plat Book C, page 143
Granted on May 1, 1770   Grant Book I, page 5

150 acres bounded on the north by William Burney.

****

Ledger, John and John Hamilton and Jean Hamilton
500 acres in St. George Parish

Granted on May 2, 1775   Grant Book M, page 1115

500 acres in Queensborough bounded on the northwest by David
Munrow.

****

Lewers, Thomas
100 acres in St. George Parish

Granted on September 6, 1774   Grant Book M, page 342

100 acres and town lot 28 in Queensborough bounded on the
west by James Balir.

****

Lewis, Benjamin
100 acres in St. George Parish

Granted on November 3, 1767   Grant Book F, page 407

100 acres bounded on the south by Daniel Douglas and land
of the said Benjamin Lewis.

****

Lewis, Benjamin
50 acres in St. George Parish

Granted on October 29, 1765   Grant Book H, page 54

50 acres bounded on the northwest by Joanna Thomas, northeast
by Thomas Irwin, southeast by ---- and west by land laid
out to Evan Lewis.

****

Lewis, Benjamin
34 acres in St. George Parish

Surveyed on November 28, 1771   Plat Book C, page 147
Granted on April 7, 1772   Grant Book H, page 76

34 acres bounded on the southwest by Evan Lewis and Jacob
Lewis, northeast by Peter Elliott and Thomas Ford and
southeast by Myrick Davies.

****

Lewis, David
150 acres in St. George Parish

Granted on September 2, 1766   Grant Book E, page 362

150 acres bounded on the south by David Emanuel.

****

Lewis, David
150 acres in St. George Parish

Granted on May 5, 1767   Grant Book F, page 238

150 acres bounded on all sides by vacant land.

****

Lewis, Evan
350 acres in St. George Parish

Surveyed on May 22, 1758   Plat Book C, page 150
Granted on August 3, 1762   Grant Book D, page 160

350 acres bounded on all sides by vacant land.

****

Lewis, Evan
150 acres in St. George Parish

Surveyed on November 27, 1766   Plat Book C, page 143
Granted on May 5, 1767   Grant Book F, page 239

150 acre tract surveyed for Evan Lewis, then ordered to Thomas
Lewis on April 7, 1767. Granted to Thomas Lewis and located
at Bryar Creek at a place called the Stalking Head Branch.

****

Lewis, Evans
100 acres in St. George Parish

Surveyed on September 15, 1772   Plat Book C, page 144
Granted on January 19, 1773   Grant Book I, page 863

100 acres bounded on the east by the said grantee and surveyed
as Evan Lewis.

****

Lewis, Francis
100 acres in St. George Parish

Surveyed on October 12, 1771   Plat Book C, page 144
Granted on July 5, 1774   Grant Book M, page 64

100 acres bounded on the north by Patrick Haragans.

****

Lewis, Henry
150 acres in St. George Parish

Surveyed on December 15, 1772   Plat Book C, page 145
Granted on September 2, 1774   Grant Book M, page 340

150 acres bounded on the east by John Duhart.

****

Lewis, Jacob
100 acres in St. George Parish

Surveyed on August 3, 1771   Plat Book C, page 146
Granted on November 5, 1771   Grant Book I, page 458

100 acres bounded on the southeast by Myrick Davis and northwest by land granted to Evan Lewis, deceased.

****

Lewis, John
100 acres in St. George Parish

Surveyed on March 23, 1773   Plat Book C, page 147
Granted on June 7, 1774   Grant Book I, page 1069

100 acres bounded on the south by land formerly of Bourington and west by William Porter.

****

Lewis, Thomas
100 acres in St. George Parish

Granted on March 3, 1767   Grant Book F, page 122

100 acres bounded on the southeast by the said Thomas Lewis.

****

Lewis, Thomas
100 acres in St. George Parish

Surveyed on October 23, 1765   Plat Book C, page 143
Granted on March 3, 1767   Grant Book F, page 124

100 acres bounded on the east by George Walker and west by the said Thomas Lewis.

****

Lewis, Thomas
150 acres in St. George Parish

Surveyed on November 27, 1766   Plat Book C, page 143
Granted on May 5, 1767   Grant Book F, page 239

150 acres located at Bryar Creek at a placed called Stalking Head Branch and surveyed for Evan Lewis and then ordered to Thomas Lewis on April 7, 1767.

****

Lewis, Thomas
200 acres in St. George Parish

Granted on February 7, 1775   Grant Book M, page 1013

200 acres bounded on the north by Evan Lewis and east by
Jacob Lewis.

*****

Lewis, Thomas
100 acres in St. George Parish

Surveyed on June 20, 1771   Plat Book C, page 143

100 acres in Queensborough bounded on the west by James Blair.

****

Lewis, William
200 acres in St. George Parish

Surveyed on March 26, 1772   Plat Book C, page 145
Granted on July 5, 1774   Grant Book M, page 63

200 acres, shown on the plat bounded on the southwest by
Beaverdam Creek.

****

Lightfoot, Philip
200 acres in St. George Parish

Surveyed on January 24, 1770   Plat Book C, page 141
Granted on June 5, 1770   Grant Book I, page 23

200 acres bounded on the southeast by John Taylor.

****

Lindall, William
100 acres in St. George Parish

Granted on December 7, 1762   Grant Book D, page 244

100 acres bounded on the northeast by the Savannah River,
southeast by John Kitt and on the northwest by James Nesmith.

****

Lindon, William
100 acres in St. George Parish

Surveyed on November 7, 1759   Plat Book C, page 143

100 acre tract surveyed for William Lindon, then ordered to
Philip Dill on April 3, 1770. Bounded on the northeast by
the Savannah River, northwest by James Nothsmith and on the
southeast by John Kitts.

****

Lindsay, Elias
100 acres in St. George Parish

Surveyed on May 6, 1769   Plat Book C, page 141
Granted on March 5, 1771   Grant Book I, page 270

100 acres bounded on all sides by vacant land.

****

Lindsey, Moses
100 acres in St. George Parish

Granted on June 2, 1767   Grant Book F, page 271

100 acres bounded on all sides by vacant land.

****

Linsey, Isaac
100 acres in St. George Parish

Granted on February 3, 1767   Grant Book F, page 67

100 acres bounded on all sides by vacant land.

****

Linsey, Thomas
100 acres in St. George Parish

Granted on October 4, 1774   Grant Book M, page 567

100 acres bounded on all sides by vacant land.

****

Litch, Thomas
100 acres in St. George Parish

Surveyed on January 8, 1761   Plat Book C, page 141
Granted on April 3, 1770   Grant Book G, page 582

100 acre tract surveyed for Thomas Litch but ordered to pass
to Joshua Odam on November 7, 1769. Granted to Joshua Odam
and bounded on the northeast by Briar Creek.

****

Little, Thomas
200 acres in St. George Parish

Surveyed on November 2, 1772   Plat Book C, page 146
Granted on October 4, 1774   Grant Book M, page 566

200 acres bounded on the southeast by David Lewis.

****

Little, William
300 acres in St. George Parish

Surveyed on November 24, 1770   Plat Book C, page 144
Granted on September 6, 1774   Grant Book M, page 341

300 acres bounded on the southwest by Samuel Gibson, northwest
by John Ingram and Adam McLeroy and on the northeast by
John Kennedy.

****

Livingstom, William
200 acres in St. George Parish

Surveyed on June 14, 1769   Plat Book C, page 140
Granted on October 3, 1769   Grant Book G, page 437

200 acres bounded on the northeast by Bud Cade.

****

Livingston, William
100 acres in St. George Parish

Surveyed on August 21, 1771   Plat Book C, page 147
Granted on March 3, 1772   Grant Book I, page 531

100 acres bounded partly on the north by Quinton Pooler, east by the said grantee and on all other sides by vacant land.

****

Lockhart, Samuel
200 acres in St. George Parish

Surveyed on August 7, 1771   Plat Book C, page 148
                                    Plat Book M, page 7
Granted on September 6, 1774   Grant Book M, page 343

200 acres bounded on all sides by vacant land.

****

Lord, Maim
100 acres in St. George Parish

Surveyed on May 3, 1769   Plat Book C, page 140

100 acres bounded on all sides by vacant land.

****

Lord, William
350 acres in St. George Parish

Granted on January 5, 1768   Grant Book G, page 10

350 acres bounded on the north by William Alexander and west by George Harnage.

****

Lord, William
100 acres in St. George Parish

Surveyed on May 3, 1769   Plat Book C, page 443
Granted on May 1, 1770   Grant Book I, page 6

100 acres bounded on the northwest partly by William Alexander, partly on the northwest and partly on the southwest by land of the said grantee.

****

Lot, John
300 acres in St. George Parish

Granted on May 7, 1765   Grant Book E, page 144

300 acres bounded on the southwest by Bryar Creek.

****

Lott, Daniel
150 acres in St. George Parish

Granted on October 29, 1765   Grant Book E, page 386

150 acres bounded on the west by Beaverdam Creek, a branch
of Buckhead Creek.

****

Lott, Daniel
100 acres in St. George Parish

Granted on October 6, 1767   Grant Book F, page 385

100 acres bounded on the east by David Cavenah.

****

Lott, John
100 acres in St. George Parish

Surveyed on November 24, 1766   Plat Book C, page 142
Granted on May 4, 1773   Grant Book I, page 979

100 acres bounded on all sides by vacant land.

****

Lott, John, Sr.
200 acres in St. George Parish

Granted on October 29, 1765   Grant Book E, page 299

200 acres bounded on the northwest by John Lott, Jr.

****

Lott, John, Sr.
100 acres in St. George Parish

Granted on December 6, 1768   Grant Book G, page 232

100 acres bounded on all sides by vacant land.

****

Lott, Mark
100 acres in St. George Parish

Surveyed on February 4, 1767   Plat Book C, page 142

100 acres bounded on the southeast by Isaac Lewis and on the southwest by Buckhead Creek.

****

Lott, Solomon
100 acres in St. George Parish

Granted on May 5, 1767   Grant Book F, page 237

100 acres bounded on all sides by vacant land.

****

Loumore, Issac and John McGee
200 acres in St. George Parish

Surveyed on September 30, 1772   Plat Book C, page 145

200 acres bounded on the north by William Moxley and south by James Simpson.

****

Lowe, James
200 acres in St. George Parish

Surveyed on June 15, 1773   Plat Book C, page 147
Granted on August 2, 1774   Grant Book M, page 213

200 acres bounded on all sides by vacant land.

****

Lowten, Elizabeth
400 acres in St. George Parish

Granted on January 3, 1775   Grant Book M, page 903

400 acres bounded on the east by Henry Irby.

****

Lowton, Reverend Timothy
600 acres in St. George Parish

Surveyed on January 29, 1772   Plat Book C, page 148
Granted on May 4, 1773   Grant Book I, page 980

600 acres bounded on the southwest by Great Ogechee River
and on the northwest by --- Savery.

****

Lowton, Reverend Timothy
300 acres in St. George Parish

Surveyed on July 27, 1773   Plat Book C, page 149

300 acres bounded on all sides by vacant land.

****

Lowton, Reverend Timothy
500 acres in St. George Parish

Surveyed on October 20, 1772   Plat Book C, page 149

500 acres bounded on all sides by vacant land.

****

Lowton, Reverend Timothy
500 acres in St. George Parish

Surveyed on October 21, 1772   Plat Book C, page 148

500 acres bounded on the north by said grantee, east by Thomas
Lewis and vacant land, and south by Thomas Yarbrough and Vacant.

****

Lowton, Reverend Timothy
400 acres in St. George Parish

Surveyed on January 31, 1772   Plat Book C, page 145

400 acres bounded on all sides by vacant land.

****

Lunday, Abraham
400 acres in St. George Parish

Original survey date unknown
Resurveyed on December 14, 1789   Plat Book M, page 5
Granted on April 13, 1761   Grant Book C, page 111

400 acres bounded on the south by Michael Paner and John
Tanner, north by Andrew Griner and east and north by the
Savannah River.

****

Lynn, Captain Thomas – Bounty
1000 acres in St. George Parish

Surveyed on April 10, 1774   Plat Book C, page 149
Granted on May 3, 1774   Grant Book I, page 1006

1000 acres bounded on the southwest by the Ogechee River.

****

Lynn, Thomas – Bounty
500 acres in St. George Parish

Granted on June 16, 1774   Grant Book I, page 1009

500 acres bounded on the southwest by Ogechee River.

****

Lynn, Thomas – Bounty
500 acres in St. George Parish

Granted on June 16, 1774   Grant Book I, page 1010

500 acres bounded on the south by the Ogechee River.

****

Lynn, Thomas – Bounty
350 acres in St. George Parish

Granted on June 16, 1774   Grant Book I, page 1011

350 acres bounded on the southwest by Ogechee River, southeast
by Reverend Timothy Lowton and northwest by the said grantee.

****

122

Lyon, John
400 acres in St. George Parish

Surveyed on December 12, 1771   Plat Book C, page 146
Granted on June 2, 1772   Grant Book I, page 635

400 acres bounded on the south by Francis Wynne, north by land
ordered ---Lindsey, and plat of survey shows Lincy.

****

Lyon, John
300 acres in St. George Parish

Surveyed on November 10, 1771   Plat Book C, page 146
Granted on June 2, 1772   Grant Book I, page 640

300 acres bounded on all sides by vacant land.

****

Lysle, Matthew
100 acres in St. George Parish

Surveyed on June 14, 1769   Plat Book C, page 140
Granted on July 3, 1770   Grant Book I, page 99

Lot 14 in the Town of Queensborough and also 100 acres in the
Township of Queensborough bounded partly on the west by
Joseph Saunders and on all other sides by vacant land.
Surveyed as Matthew Lyle.

****

Mackay, John
200 acres in St. George Parish

Granted on May 5, 1767   Grant Book F, page 245

200 acres bounded on all sides by vacant land.

****

Mainer, John
300 acres in St. George Parish

Surveyed on January 10, 1760   Plat Book C, page 404
Granted on November 6, 1764   Grant Book E, page 73

300 acres bounded on the northeast by Savannah River.

Mainer, William
300 acres in St. George Parish

Surveyed on May 25, 1761   Plat Book C, page 402
Granted on November 6, 1764   Grant Book E, page 76

300 acres bounded on the north by Savannah River, northwest
by Richard Wallis and northeast by William Cochran.

****

Mainer, William
100 acres in St. George Parish

Surveyed on September 14, 1761   Plat Book C, page 402
Granted on November 6, 1764   Grant Book E, page 77

100 acres bounded on the northeast by a great pond.

****

Maithland, Thomas
50 acres in St. George Parish

Surveyed on February 18, 1772   Plat Book C, page 202
Granted on January 3, 1775   Grant Book M, page 908

50 acres bounded on all sides by vacant land.

****

Man, John
100 acres in St. George Parish

Granted on September 2, 1766   Grant Book E, page 406

100 acres bounded on the west by Spring Branch and said Man.

****

Mann, John
150 acres in St. George Parish

Surveyed on November 21, 1767   Plat Book C, pages 193 & 220
Granted on August 2, 1768   Grant Book G, page 159

150 acres bounded on the southwest by Beaverdam Creek.

****

Mann, John
150 acres in St. George Parish

Surveyed on February 7, 1769   Plat Book C, page 194
Granted on March 7, 1769   Grant Book G, page 282

150 acres bounded on the northeast by John Grant, southwest
and partly southeast by Edward Barnard.

****

Mann, John
300 acres in St. George Parish

Surveyed on May 28, 1759   Plat Book C, page 400

300 acres bounded on the north by Samuel Gandy.

****

Marin, David
200 acres in St. George Parish

Surveyed on November 20, 1770   Plat Book C, page 199
Granted on May 7, 1771   Grant Book I, page 315

200 acres in Queensborough Township bounded on the southeast
by James Waters.

****

Marks, Richard
85 acres in St. George Parish

Surveyed on August 12, 1768   Plat Book C, page 193

85 acres bounded on the northwest by Joseph Warnet, east by
Savannah River and south by William Bland.

****

Marshall, John
100 acres in St. George Parish

Surveyed on February 1, 1772   Plat Book C, page 203
Granted on August 2, 1774   Grant Book M, page 234

100 acres in Queensborough bounded on the northeast by Alexander
Chesnut, northwest by Quinton Pooler, and on the south corner
by George Galphin.

****

Marshall, Joseph
400 acres in St. George Parish

Surveyed on March 8, 1770   Plat Book M, page 44
Granted on July 5, 1774   Grant Book M, page 74

400 acres in Queensborough bounded on the northeast by William McConkey.

****

Marshall, John
100 acres in St. George Parish

Granted on July 5, 1774   Grant Book M, page 75

100 acres bounded on the southwest by Ogechee River and on the southeast by George Galphin.

****

Marshall, Matthew
100 acres in St. George Parish

Surveyed on July 11, 1770   Plat Book C, page 199
Granted on February 5, 1771   Grant Book I, page 254

100 acres in Queensborough bounded on all sides by vacant land.

****

Martin, James
100 acres in St. George Parish

Granted on April 7, 1767   Grant Book F, page 197

100 acres bounded on all sides by vacant land.

****

Martin, James
100 acres in St. George Parish

Surveyed on June 15, 1769   Plat Book C, page 196
Granted on August 7, 1770   Grant Book I, page 76

100 acres bounded on the northwest by Ogechee River.

****

Martin, James
100 acres in St. George Parish

Surveyed on May 27, 1772   Plat Book C, page 209
Granted on August 2, 1774   Grant Book M, page 229

100 acres in Queensborough bounded on the north by Robert
Warnock and vacant land, west by John Martin, south by Joseph
Beatty and vacant land and east by vacant land; and also
Town Lot 76 in Queensborough.

****

Martin, John
400 acres in St. George Parish

Surveyed on June 27, 1769   Plat Book C, page 191
Granted on July 3, 1770   Grant Book I, page 100

400 acres in the Township of Queensborough and also Town
Lot 30 in the said town.

****

Martin, Oilver
150 acres in St. George Parish

Granted on April 7, 1767   Grant Book F, page 194

150 acres bounded on all sides by vacant land.

****

Maxwell, Audley
150 acres in St. George Parish

Granted on September 6, 1774   Grant Book M, page 356

150 acres bounded on the north by William Pannell and south
by unknown land.

****

Maxwell, Audley
350 acres in St. George Parish

Granted on February 7, 1775   Grant Book M, page 1029

350 acres bounded on the south by Isaac Wimberley and west
by William Pennell.

****

Maxwell, James
500 acres in St. George Parish

Surveyed on June 15, 1773   Plat Book C, page 207
Granted on January 3, 1775   Grant Book M, page 916

500 acres bounded on the southeast by Christopher Clark,
Fitz and Charles Lamb, southwest by John Revers and vacant
land. The plat shows Thomas Lamb instead of Charles.

****

Maxwell, Thomas
350 acres in St. George Parish

Granted on September 1, 1767   Grant Book F, page 356

350 acres bounded on the north by the said Thomas Maxwell.

****

Mayer, Michael
100 acres in St. George Parish

Granted on June 2, 1772   Grant Book I, page 628

100 acres bounded on all sides by vacant land.

****

McBride, Samuel
300 acres in St. George Parish

Surveyed on April 18, 1770   Plat Book C, page 195
Granted on November 6, 1770   Grant Book I, page 208

300 acres in Queensborough Township and bounded on the southeast by James Finley.

****

McBride, Thomas
150 acres in St. George Parish

Surveyed on December 22, 1770   Plat Book C, page 200
Granted on September 6, 1774   Grant Book M, page 353

150 acres in Queensborough bounded on the northeast by Samuel
McBride.

****

McCalvey, James
100 acres in St. George Parish

Surveyed on June 10, 1769   Plat Book C, page 192
Granted on July 3, 1770   Grant Book I, page 105

100 acres in Queensborough Township bounded on the west by
David Green, east by land of McKay, north by Matthew Moore,
and south by the Town Common; and also Town Lot 31 in
Queensborough.

****

McCanlis, John
200 acres in St. George Parish

Surveyed on November 20, 1770   Plat Book C, page 199
Granted on September 6, 1774   Grant Book M, page 363

200 acres in Queensborough bounded on the southeast by James
Fleming, southwest by George Donelson and southeast by James
Beatty.

****

McClendgan
150 acres in St. George Parish

Surveyed on August 12, 1772   Plat Book C, page 203
Granted on August 2, 1774   Grant Book M, page 224

150 acres in Queensborough bounded on the northwest by -- Crossley

****

McCollum, John
200 acres in St. George Parish

Granted on June 7, 1757   Grant Book A, page 488

200 acres in the District of Halifax bounded on all sides
by vacant land.

****

McConky, Edward
350 acres in St. George Parish

Surveyed on January 8, 1771   Plat Book C, page 200
Granted on September 6, 1774   Grant Book M, page 358

350 acres in Queensborough bounded on the northwest by
James Fleming.

****

McConkey, William
100 acres in St. George Parish

Surveyed on June 24, 1769   Plat Book C, page 191
Granted on July 3, 1770   Grant Book I, page 104

100 acres in the Township of Queensborough and also Town
Lot 72 in Queensborough.

****

McCormick, John
100 acres in St. George Parish

Surveyed on November 8, 1770   Plat Book C, page 209

100 acres bounded on all sides by vacant land.

****

McCormick, Patrick
100 acres in St. George Parish

Surveyed on October 29, 1770   Plat Book C, page 198
Granted on May 7, 1771   Grant Book I, page 316

100 acres bounded on all sides by vacant land.

****

McCormick, Robert
250 acres in St. George Parish

Granted on February 7, 1775   Grant Book M, page 1027

250 acres bounded on the northeast by James Gray and Thomas
Shruder and the Savannah River, and northwest by Jonathon
Bulkey.

****

McCorrie, Anderson
300 acres in St. George Parish

Granted on January 5, 1768   Grant Book G, page 12

300 acres bounded on the south by William Webb, north and west by John Gasper Greiner and northeast by the Savannah River.

****

McCroan, Thomas
250 acres in St. George Parish

Surveyed on March 19, 1773   Plat Book C, page 206
Granted on October 4, 1774   Grant Book M, page 574

250 acres in Queensborough bounded on the southwest by John Howell.

****

McCulugh, Patrick
100 acres in St. George Parish

Surveyed on February 20, 1770   Plat Book C, page 202
Granted on September 6, 1774   Grant Book M, page 347

100 acres in Queensborough bounded on the east by Robert Garvin and on the southwest by Matthew Lysle.

****

McCurrie, Andrew
100 acres in St. George Parish

Granted on April 13, 1761   Grant Book C, page 166

100 acres bounded on the east by Savannah River, north by Greiner and south by Richard Hubbard.

****

McCurrie, Andrew
100 acres partly in St. Matthew and partly in St. George Parish

Granted on February 5, 1765   Grant Book E, page 114

100 acres located on both sides of Beaverdam Creek at a place known as the Great Springs, 75 miles from Savannah and bounded on all sides by vacant land.

****

McCurrie, Andrew
300 acres in St. George Parish

Granted on February 5, 1765   Grant Book E, page 115

300 acres located 71 miles from Savannah on the north side
of Bryar Creek, bounded on the southwest by Bryar Creek.

****

McCurrie, Andrew
100 acres in St. George Parish

Granted on May 5, 1767   Grant Book F, page 247

100 acres bounded on the northwest by John Branson, northeast and southeast by Henry Overstreet, Jr., southwest by
land vacant; which tract was heretofore ordered to John
McNish, co-partner of the said Andrew McCurrie.

****

McDonald, George
250 acres in St. George Parish

Granted on October 6, 1767   Grant Book F, page 384

250 acres at a place called the Dry Branch.

****

McDonald, George
150 acres in St. George Parish

Surveyed on April 26, 1768   Plat Book C, page 193
Granted on October 4, 1768   Grant Book G, page 199

150 acres bounded on the northwest by John Large and on the
south by the said George McDonald.

****

McDonald, William
400 acres in St. George Parish

Granted on October 2, 1759   Grant Book B, page 223

400 acres bounded on the east by Savannah River and on the
north and south by Itensler and Meyer.

****

McDonald, William
200 acres in St. George Parish

Surveyed on December 11, 1760   Plat Book C, page 196 & 236
Granted on August 3, 1762   Grant Book D, page 167

200 acres on the Savannah River opposite Pukins Bluff and
bounded on the northeast by Savannah River and northwest by
Samuel Moore.

****

McDonald, William
250 acres in St. George Parish

Granted on September 1, 1767   Grant Book F, page 359

250 acres bounded on the northeast by William McDonald and
Samuel Moore and on the northwest by Samuel Moore and James
Nessmith.

****

McDonald, William
350 acres in St. George Parish

Granted on April 5, 1768   Grant Book G, page 82

350 acres bounded on the northeast by the said William
McDonald and James Nesmyth.

****

McDonals, William
200 acres in St. George Parish

Granted on September 3, 1765   Grant Book E, page 237

200 acres bounded on the northeast by the Savannah River and
northwest by the said grantee.

****

McGee, John and Isaac Loumore
200 acres in St. George Parish

Surveyed on September 30, 1772   Plat Book C, page 145

200 acres bounded on the north by William Moxley and south
by James Simpson.

****

McGee, Patrick
100 acres in St. George Parish

Surveyed on February 26, 1771   Plat Book C, page 201
Granted on November 1, 1774   Grant Book M, page 702

100 acres in Queensborough bounded on the northeast by
James Hamilton.

****

McGilivray and Clark (no given names shown)
50 acres in St. George Parish

Surveyed on May 18, 1758   Plat Book C, page 400

50 acres bounded on the southwest by Bryer Creek.

****

McGillivray, Alexander
100 acres in St. George Parish

Granted on February 3, 1762   Grant Book D, page 42

100 acres bounded on all sides by vacant lnad.

****

McGillavray, Lachlan
1000 acres in St. George Parish

Granted on July 7, 1761   Grant Book C, page 150

1000 acres bounded on the east by Savannah River and south
by David Douglass.

****

McGillivray, Lachlan
500 acres in St. George Parish

Granted on September 6, 1768   Grant Book G, page 185

500 acres bounded on the north by John Mann and supposed to
adjoin southerly by said Lachlan McGillivray.

****

McGown, David
100 acres in St. George Parish

Surveyed on November 20, 1770   Plat Book C, page 199
Granted on October 1, 1771   Grant Book I, page 433

100 acres in Queensborough Township bounded on the northeast
by Thomas Wighan.

****

McGuffock, William
100 acres in St. George Parish

Surveyed on February 10, 1773   Plat Book C, page 201
Granted on November 1, 1774   Grant Book M, page 713

100 acres bounded on the south by Margaret Wilson.

****

McHenry, James
150 acres in St. George Parish

Granted on July 1, 1760   Grant Book B, page 397

150 acres bounded on the south by William Green and on the
northwest by John Clarke.

****

McHenry, James
300 acres in St. George Parish

Granted on October 4, 1763   Grant Book D, page 338

300 acres bounded on the east by the Savannah River, south by
James Germany and northwest by John Davis.

****

McHenry, James
250 acres in St. George Parish

Surveyed on August 27, 1761   Plat Book C, page 403
Granted on October 2, 1764   Grant Book E, page 43

250 acres bounded on the east by a lagoon, south by Savannah
River and John Bradley, west by vacant and north by heirs of

Remigins Van Munch.

****

McKay, James
300 acres in St. George Parish

Surveyed on May 18, 1761   Plat Book C, page 400
Granted on May 21, 1762   Grant Book D, page 101

300 acres bounded on the northeast by the Savannah River.

****

McKay, James
100 acres in St. George Parish

Surveyed on July 1, 1769   Plat Book C, page 197
Granted on August 2, 1774   Grant Book M, page 230

100 acres bounded on the northeast by the Savannah River,
northwest by Kelsall and Munroe and southeast by the
said James McKay.

****

McKay, Robert and Thomas Netherclift
1000 acres in St. George Parish

Granted on October 4, 1774   Grant Book M, page 581

100 acres bounded on the south by the Great Ogechee River.

****

McKewen, James
100 acres in St. George Parish

Surveyed on August 20, 1770   Plat Book C, page 200
Granted on March 7, 1775   Grant Book M, page 1084

100 acres bounded on all sides by vacant land.

****

McLean, John
500 acres in St. George Parish

Granted on March 3, 1767   Grant Book F, page 131

500 acres bounded on the southeast and northeast by Nathan Hooker.

****

136

McLeroy, Adam
150 acres in St. George Parish

Surveyed on June 19, 1769   Plat Book C, page 197
Granted on July 3, 1770   Grant Book I, page 103

150 acres in Queensborough Township bounded on the southeast
by Black Jack Creek and southwest by Robert Sampson, and
also Town Lot 45 in Queensborough.

****

McMurphy, Daniel
100 acres in St. George Parish

Granted on March 3, 1772   Grant Book I, page 537

100 acres bounded on the southwest by James Finley.

****

McNail, Daniel
150 acres in St. George Parish

Surveyed on June 18, 1770   Plat Book C, page 186
Granted on November 6, 1770   Grant Book I, page 211

150 acres in Queensborough Township bounded on the southeast by Great Creek and also Town Lot 1 in Queensborough.

****

McQueen, James
100 acres in St. George Parish

Surveyed on October 24, 1772   Plat Book C, page 205
Granted on January 19, 1773   Grant Book I, page 868

100 acres bounded on the east by the grantee and west by
Thomas Miller.

****

McQueen, John
500 acres in St. George Parish

Surveyed on April 12, 1773   Plat Book C, page 206

500 acres bounded on the southeast by the said John McQueen,
southwest by Briar Creek and northwest by said John McQueen.

****

McQueen, John
500 acres in St. George Parish

Surveyed on April 12, 1773   Plat Book C, page 208

500 acres bounded on the southeast by the said John McQueen
and southwest by Briar Creek.

****

McQueen, John
500 acres in St. George Parish

Surveyed on April 12, 1773   Plat Book C, page 207

500 acres bounded on the southwest by Briar Creek and northwest by the said John McQueen.

****

Mercer, John
200 acres in St. George Parish

Surveyed on February 2, 1767   Plat Book C, page 195
Granted on April 3, 1770   Grant Book G, page 581

200 acres bounded on the southeast by James Bennett. Plat
says bounded on the southwest by Beaverdam Creek.

****

Meyer, Michael
100 acres in St. George Parish

Surveyed on February 20, 1769   Plat Book C, page 194

100 acres bounded on all sides by vacnat land.

****

Mezell, David
100 acres in St. George Parish

Surveyed on January 24, 1771   Plat Book C, page 200
Granted on November 1, 1774   Grant Book M, page 685

100 acres bounded on all sides by vacnat land.

****

Milledge, John
650 acres in St. George Parish

Granted on November 2, 1762   Grant Book D, page 232

650 acres bounded by the Savannah River on the northeast and
northwest by James Love and lying on the southeast and
northwest of 100 acres of land formerly laid out for Joseph
Parker.

****

Milledge, John
100 acres in St. George Parish

Granted on November 2, 1762   Grant Book D, page 233

100 acres formerly allotted Joseph Parker and by him sold to
the said John Milledge bounded on the northeast by the
Savannah River and on every other side by the said John
Milledge.

****

Milledge, Mary Elizabeth
400 acres in St. George Parish

Granted on November 1, 1774   Grant Book M, page 690

400 acres bounded on the north by Frances Robe and east by
John Earle.

****

Miller, Elias
200 acres in St. George Parish

Granted on June 2, 1767   Grant Book F, page 273

200 acres on the north side of Briar Creek and bounded on the
southwest by Briar Creek and northwest by Andrew McCorrie.

****

Miller, Michael
100 acres in St. George Parish

Surveyed on October 23, 1771   Plat Book C, page 205

100 acres bounded on the west by Patrick Butler, northeast by William Pilcher and southwest by Edward Pilcher.

****

Miller, Nathaniel
300 acres in St. George Parish

Granted on October 2, 1764   Grant Book E, page 51

300 acres bounded on all sides by vacant land.

****

Miller, Nathaniel
250 acres in St. George Parish

Surveyed on January 1, 1760   Plat Book C, page 400
Granted on November 6, 1764   Grant Book E, page 64

250 acres bounded on the west by the said Nathaniel Miller, east by the Savannah River, south by Edward Barnard and north by William Colsen.

****

Miller, Nathaniel
100 acres in St. George Parish

Surveyed on July 9, 1771   Plat Book C, page 203
Granted on September 6, 1774   Grant Book M, page 359

100 acres bounded on the east by Champ and Neal.

****

Miller, Nathaniel
200 acres in St. George Parish

Surveyed on October 2, 1771   Plat Book C, page 204
Granted on September 6, 1774   Grant Book M, page 361

200 acres bounded on all sides by vacant land.

****

Miller, Nathaniel
79 acres in St. Matthew and St. George Parish

Surveyed on August 26, 1768   Plat Book C, page 195

79 acres bounded on the north by Johnson, Wylly and Nathaniel Miller, west by Johnson and Wylly, south by Johnson, Wylly and Company and east by Miller and Company.

****

Miller, Nicholas
100 acres in St. George Parish

Granted on March 3, 1772   Grant Book I, page 538

100 acres bounded on the northeast by William Pilcher.

****

Miller, Richard
100 acres in St. George Parish

Surveyed on November 22, 1763   Plat Book C, page 198

100 acres bounded on all sides by vacant lands.

****

Miller, Robert
100 acres in St. George Parish

Surveyed on November 20, 1772   Plat Book C, page 208
Granted on June 7, 1774   Grant Book I, page 1072

100 acres bounded on the south by John Thomas.

****

Mills, George
50 acres in St. George Parish

Granted on October 6, 1772   Grant Book H, page 89

50 acres bounded on the east by James Ogelvies.

****

Mincely, John
250 acres in St. George Parish

Granted on January 3, 1775   Grant Book M, page 915

250 acres in Queensborough bounded on the southwest by
David Morrow, northwest by Perkinson and northeast by
John Wilson.

****

Minis, Philip
500 acres in St. George Parish

Surveyed on July 4, 1773   Plat Book C, page 205
Granted on June 7, 1774   Grant Book I, page 1041

500 acres bounded on the southwest by Buckhead and northwest by Bennett's land.

****

Mobley, Thomas
300 acres in St. George Parish

Surveyed on September 26, 1768   Plat Book C, page 198

300 acres bounded on the northwest by Thomas Cuadrey and
on the northeast by Peter Landon.

****

Mobley, William
300 acres in St. George Parish

Surveyed on October 12, 1769   Plat Book C, page 193
Granted on September 6, 1774   Grant Book M, page 362

300 acres bounded on the southeast and northeast by Thomas
Mabley and John Burnsides and northwest by William Williams.

****

Monson, John
250 acres in St. George Parish

Surveyed on June 28, 1773   Plat Book C, page 209
Granted on September 6, 1774   Grant Book M, page 357

142

250 acres in Queensborough Township bounded on the north by Reedy Branch and Francis Mountain, south by John Allen, John Gilmore and Thomas Beatty, east by John Bartholomew and James Thomson and west by John Allan and vacant land, and also Town Lot 82 in Queensborough.

****

Montgomery, Barrott
200 acres in St. George Parish

Granted on November 3, 1767   Grant Book F, page 409

200 acres bounded on the northeast by Bryar Creek.

****

Moody, Benjamin
400 acres in St. George Parish

Granted on August 6, 1765   Grant Book E, page 203

400 acres bounded on the southeast by John Conyers.

****

Moore, Aaron
150 acres in St. George Parish

Granted on June 7, 1757   Grant Book A, page 456

150 acres in the District of Halifax and bounded on the north by the Savannah River.

****

Moore, John
150 acres in St. George Parish

Surveyed on June 2, 1765   Plat Book C, page 197

150 acres bounded on all sides by vacant land.

****

Moore, Joseph
200 acres in St. George Parish

Surveyed on March 4, 1772   Plat Book C, page 208
Granted on May 4, 1773   Grant Book I, page 982

200 acres bounded on the north by Briar Creek and on the west by Thomas Whitehead.

****

Moore, Matthew
250 acres in St. George Parish

Surveyed on June 10, 1769   Plat Book C, page 192
Granted on July 3, 1770   Grant Book I, page 106

250 acres in Queensborough Township bounded on the west by Rudy Branch, south by James McCalvey, east by James McKay and north by James Hadin and Joseph Saunders, and also Town Lot 5 in the Town of Queensborough.

****

Moore, Samuel
300 acres in St. George Parish

Surveyed on December 12, 1760   Plat Book C, page 410
Granted on August 3, 1762   Grant Book D, page 166

300 acres bounded on the southeast by William McDonald, northwest by James Nesmith and northeast by the Savannah River.

****

Moore, William
250 acres in St. George Parish

Granted on May 5, 1767   Grant Book F, page 242

250 acres bounded on all sides by vacant land.

****

Morel, John
300 acres in St. George Parish

Granted on January 3, 1775   Grant Book M, page 912

300 acres bounded on the northeast by Benjamin Horn.

****

Morel, John
500 acres in St. George Parish

Granted on February 7, 1775   Grant Book M, page 1033

500 acres bounded on all sides by vacant land.

****

Morgan, Robert
250 acres in St. George Parish

Surveyed on September 5, 1768   Plat Book C, page 195
Granted on July 5, 1774   Grant Book M, page 76

250 acres located at a place known as the Cool Spring Branch.

****

Morgan, Thomas
1000 acres in St. George Parish

Granted on April 2, 1765   Grant Book E, page 130

1000 acres located on Bryar Creek, 81 miles from Savannah.

****

Morgan, Thomas
100 acres in St. George Parish

Surveyed on February 16, 1767   Plat Book M, page 59
Granted on September 1, 1767   Grant Book F, page 361

100 acres bounded on the east by Lachlan McGillivray and
south by Neal McDavid.

****

Morgan, Thomas
300 acres in St. George Parish

Surveyed on January 23, 1771   Plat Book C, page 198
Granted on October 1, 1771   Grant Book I, page 436

300 acres bounded on the northeast by Savannah River, northwest
by Darby Kennedy and southeast by William Handley.

****

Morris, John
200 acres in St. George Parish

Granted on June 5, 1765   Grant Book E, page 167

200 acres includes the Walnut Springs on Buckhead Creek.

****

Morris, John
100 acres in St. George Parish

Granted on September 3, 1765   Grant Book E, page 236

100 acres bounded on the north by John McClom and William Moore.

****

Morris, John
100 acres in St. George Parish

Granted on October 6, 1767   Grant Book F, page 388

100 acres bounded on the west and south by Jacob Kettle and
John Warnock and southeast by John McClain.

****

Morrison, Adam
200 acres in St. George Parish

Surveyed on June 19, 1769   Plat Book C, page 192
Granted on July 3, 1770   Grant Book I, page 101

200 acres in Queensborough Township bounded on the west by
Black Jack Branch and John Morrison and also Town Lot 32 in
the Town of Queensborough.

****

Morrison, John
100 acres in St. George Parish

Surveyed on June 19, 1769   Plat Book C, page 192
Granted on July 3, 1770   Grant Book I, page 102

100 acres in the Township of Queensborough bounded on the east
by Black Jack Branch and Adam Morrison and Town Lot 15 in
the Town of Queensborough.

****

Morrison, John
50 acres in St. George Parish

Surveyed on April 14, 1772   Plat Book C, page 203
Granted on August 2, 1774   Grant Book M, page 225

50 acres in Queensborough Township bounded on the northwest
by Manuel, east by William and John Gibson and southwest
by James Fleming.

****

Morrow, David
100 acres in St. George Parish

Granted on September 6, 1774   Grant Book M, page 354

100 acres in Queensborough Township and bounded on the north
by David Holmes, southwest by Parkinson and west by Lamberts
Creek.

****

Morrow, David
150 acres in St. George Parish

Granted on September 6, 1774   Grant Book M, page 355

150 acres in Queensborough Township bounded on the northeast
by Parkinson and the said David Morrow and northeast by John
McNiely.

****

Moses, Philip
150 acres in St. George Parish

Surveyed on October 23, 1772   Plat Book C, page 204
Granted on April 6, 1773   Grant Book I, page 955

150 acres bounded on the southeast by Emanuel.

****

Mounsey, Isaac
100 acres in St. George Parish

Surveyed on July 19, 1771   Plat Book C, page 203
Granted on October 4, 1774   Grant Book M, page 573

100 acres bounded on the northeast by Elijah Brazeal.

****

Mountain, Francis
300 acres in St. George Parish

Surveyed on November 11, 1772   Plat Book C, page 202
Granted on September 6, 1774   Grant Book M, page 348

300 acres in Queensborough Township bounded on all sides by vacant land.

****

Moxley, Thomas
300 acres in St. George Parish

Granted on December 6, 1768   Grant Book G, page 237

300 acres bounded on the northwest by Thomas Caildrey and northeast by Peter Landon.

****

Moxley, William
400 acres in St. George Parish

Surveyed on September 19, 1762   Plat Book C, page 194
Granted on December 6, 1768   Grant Book G, page 235

400 acres bounded on the south by Luke Dean and William Pendrys and northwest by Thomas Graham.

****

Moxley, William
100 acres in St. George Parish

Surveyed on March 22, 1773   Plat Book C, page 201

100 acres bounded on the northeast by Samuel Little, southeast by Isaac Larimore and on the southwest by James Black.

****

Muir, John
500 acres in St. George Parish

Surveyed on June 9, 1772   Plat Book C, page 206
Granted on January 5, 1773 Grant Book I, page 831

500 acres bounded on the south by Moses Nunes.

****

Mulkey, John
100 acres in St. George Parish

Surveyed on July 2, 1766   Plat Book C, page 196
Granted on August 1, 1769 Grant Book G, page 391

100 acres bounded on all sides by vacant land.

****

Mulkey, John
150 acres in St. George Parish

Surveyed on August 8, 1771 Plat Book C, page 204

150 acres bounded on the northeast by Thomas Leeth and on
the southwest by William Green.

****

Mulkey, Jonathon
329 acres in St. George Parish

Granted on March 5, 1765   Grant Book E, page 119

329 acres bounded on the northeast by the Savannah River
and on the northwest by Jonathon Mulkey.

****

Mulkey, Jonathon
1000 acres in St. George Parish

Surveyed on May 4, 1767   Plat Book C, page 196
Granted on June 6, 1769   Grant Book G, page 336

1000 acres which includes 100 acres heretofore ordered said
Mulkey and bounded on the north by Owen O'Daniel and east by
the said Jonathon Mulkey.

****

Mulkey, Jonathon
100 acres in St. George Parish

Surveyed on June 3, 1769   Plat Book C, page 194
Granted on March 7, 1775   Grant Book M, page 1082

100 acres bounded on all sides by vacant land.

****

Mulkey, Moses
100 acres in St. George Parish

Surveyed on March 18, 1767   Plat Book C, page 182
Granted on September 6, 1774   Grant Book M, page 364

100 acres bounded on the southeast by James Gray, southwest
by Briar Creek and surveyed as in St. Paul Parish.

****

Mullryne, Catherine
550 acres part in St. Matthews and part in St. George

Granted on April 7, 1767   Grant Book F, page 192

550 acres bounded on the east by land ordered Lewis Johnson
and Alexander Wylly, north partly by John Conyers and on
every other side by vacant land.

****

Mullryne, John
500 acres part in St. Matthews and part in St. George

Granted on April 7, 1767   Grant Book F, page 191

500 acres bounded on the south by Josiah Tatnell.

****

Mullryne, John
200 acres part in St. Matthew and part in St. George

Granted on September 1, 1767   Grant Book F, page 353

200 acres bounded on the south and east by Catherine Mullryne, north by Josiah Tatnell and on every other side by vacant land, which tract was heretofore ordered and surveyed for John Conyers.

****

Munro, Simon and Roger Kelsall
1000 acres in St. George Parish

Surveyed on September 25, 1766   Plat Book C, page 121
Granted on February 2, 1768   Grant Book G, page 24

1000 acres bounded on the northeast partly by Philip Alston and partly by John Waters. Plat shows Alexander Lamar also bounding on the northeast.

****

Munro, Simon and Roger Kelsall
100 acres in St. George Parish

Surveyed on September 24, 1766   Plat Book C, page 121
Granted on February 2, 1768   Grant Book G, page 26

100 acres bounded on the north by the Savannah River.

****

Munro, Simon and Roger Kelsall
200 acres in St. George Parish

Surveyed on October 27, 1766   Plat Book C, page 121
Granted on March 1, 1768   Grant Book G, page 51

200 acres bounded on the north by Zachariah Fenn, northeast by Philip Alston and southeast by Alexander Lamar.

****

Munro, Simon and Roger Kelsall
100 acres in St. George Parish

Granted on March 1, 1768   Grant Book G, page 52

100 acres bounded on the northeast by Zachariah Fenn and south-east by Alexander Lamar.

****

151

Murphey, James
100 acres in St. George Parish

Granted on October 29, 1765   Grant Book E, page 308

100 acres bounded on all sides by vacant land.

****

Murphey, John
150 acres in St. George Parish

Surveyed on September 20, 1769   Plat Book C, page 197
Granted on February 6, 1770   Grant Book G, page 526

150 acres bounded on all sides by vacant land.

****

Murphrey, Wright
450 acres in St. George Parish

Surveyed on July 18, 1771   Plat Book C, page 123
                                   Plat Book M, page 127
Granted on December 3, 1771   Grant Book I, page 479

450 acres resurveyed on November 19, 1827 for Wright Murphrey
and found to contain 500 acres.

****

Murphy, William
100 acres in St. George Parish

Granted on April 5, 1768   Grant Book G, page 81

100 acres bounded on all sides by vacant land.

****

Murray, David
150 acres in St. George Parish

Surveyed on November 1, 1771   Plat Book C, page 204
Granted on August 2, 1774   Grant Book M, page 228

150 acres bounded on the north by Stephen Murray.

****

Murray, John
100 acres in St. George Parish

Surveyed on November 2, 1771   Plat Book C, page 202
Granted on September 6, 1774   Grant Book M, page 349

100 acres bounded on all sides by vacant land.

****

Murray, Stephen
100 acres in St. George Parish

Surveyed on August 29, 1770   Plat Book C, page 201
Granted on July 2, 1771   Grant Book I, page 367

100 acres bounded on the northwest by Edward Barnard.

****

Musick, Ambs.
150 acres in St. George Parish

Surveyed on December 16, 1771   Plat Book C, page 201

150 acres bounded on the south and east by Ogechee River.

****

Muster, James
200 acres in St. George Parish

Granted on February 5, 1765   Grant Book E, page 102

200 acres of land heretofore ordered to Caleb Howell who has not taken out the grant for it. Bounded on the northeast by Briar Creek and southeast by Hugh Kennedy.

****

Napper, John
100 acres in St. George Parish

Surveyed on December 8, 1772   Plat Book M, page 64
Granted on October 4, 1774   Grant Book M, page 586

100 acres bounded on the south by Ogechee River, west by Daniel Douglass and east by William Simpson.

****

Neal, Charles
100 acres in St. George Parish

Granted on April 5, 1763   Grant Book D, page 300

100 acres bounded on the east by the Savannah River, northwest by James Thomas and southeast by John Davis.

****

Nelson, John and Thomas Nelson
150 acres in St. George Parish

Granted on April 7, 1767   Grant Book F, page 198

150 acres on Walnut Branch and at the time of survey was bounded
by vacant land, which said tract was heretofore ordered John
Nelson, father of the said John and Thomas Nelson who died
before he had perfected his grant.

****

Nelson, Thomas and John Nelson
150 acres in St. Georgia Parish

Granted on April 7, 1767   Grant Book F, page 198

150 acres on Walnut Creek and at the time of survey was
bounded on every side by vacant land, which said tract was
heretofore ordered John Nelson, father of the said John
and Thomas Nelson, who died before the grant was perfected.

****

Nesmith, James
150 acres in St. George Parish

Surveyed on December 13, 1760   Plat Book C, page 414
Granted on November 6, 1764   Grant Book E, page 65

150 acres bounded on northeast by Savannah River, southeast by
James Nesmith. Original warrant says tract located about
four miles below Stoney Bluff.

****

Nesmith, James
250 acres in St. George Parish

Granted on November 6, 1764   Grant Book E, page 66

250 acres bounded on the southeast by William Lindall, northwest by vacant land and the said James Nesmith.

****

Nesmith, James
100 acres in St. George Parish

Granted on November 4, 1766   Grant Book E, page 400

100 acres bounded on the northwest by Samuel Moo (?), northeast by said James Nesmith and southeast by Peter Randan.

****

Netherclift, Thomas
500 acres in St. George Parish

Surveyed on March 15, 1769   Plat Book M, page 39
Granted on June 6, 1769   Grant Book G, page 340

500 acres bounded on the northeast by the said Thomas Netherclift, southeast by James Habersham and Charles Burnett. The
grant shows no parish location but the plat shows St. George.

****

Netherclift, Thomas
500 acres in St. George Parish

Surveyed on March 15, 1769   Plat Book M, page 39
Granted on June 6, 1769   Grant Book G, page 341

500 acres bounded on the northwest by the said Thomas Netherclift and southeast by Charles Burnett. The grant shows no
parish location but the plat shows St. George.

****

Netherclift, Thomas
300 acres in St. George Parish

Granted on December 6, 1774   Grant Book M, page 818

300 acres bounded on the northeast by land ordered one Eastlick and land of Josiah Dickson, south by Samuel Lockhard and vacant, west by Henry Sharp and east by land ordered John Good.

****

Netherclift, Thomas and Robert McKay
1000 acres in St. George Parish

Granted on October 4, 1774   Grant Book M, page 581

1000 acres bounded on the south by the Great Ogechee.

****

Nevill, John
100 acres in St. George Parish

Granted on June 5, 1771   Grant Book I, page 346

100 acres bounded on the northwest by Gilshot Thomas and on the southwest by Briar Creek.

****

Nichols, James
300 acres in St. George Parish

Granted on July 5, 1774   Grant Book M, page 79

300 acres bounded on the west and north by Thomas Yarborough and south by Christian Camford.

****

Nicholson, Thomas
100 acres in St. George Parish

Granted on November 1, 1774   Grant Book M, page 715

100 acres bounded on the northwest by Revd. Timothy Louten and southeast by John Powell.

****

Oadam, Frederick
200 acres in St. George Parish

200 acres in St. George Parish

Granted on May 5, 1767   Grant Book F, page 252

200 acres bounded on the north partly by Bryar Creek and on every other side by vacant land.

****

Oadam, William
100 acres in St. George Parish

Granted on October 6, 1767   Grant Book F, page 390

100 acres bounded on all sides by vacant land.

****

Oates, John
300 acres in St. George Parish

Granted on August 2, 1774   Grant Book M, page 237

300 acres bounded on the southwest by the Ogechee River.

****

O'Bryan, David
100 acres in St. George Parish

Granted on May 5, 1767   Grant Book F, page 251

100 acres on north side of Briar Creek bounded on the east by Timothy O'Bryan and west by Abraham Lunday.

****

O'Bryan, Timothy
400 acres in St. George Parish

Surveyed on December 12, 1765   Original plat only
Granted on May 5, 1767   Grant Book F, page 250

400 acres on north side of Bryar Creek bounded on south by Briar Creek, west by David O'Bryan and east by John Brunson. The original plat of survey is on file in the Surveyor General Department and not recorded.

****

O'Bryan, William, Jr.
600 acres in St. George Parish

Granted on January 3, 1775   Grant Book M, page 923

600 acres bounded on the northeast by Richard Capers and vacant,
southeast by Great Ogechee River and west by Francis Jenkins.

****

O'Cain, Daniel
300 acres in St. George Parish

Granted on November 6, 1764   Grant Book E, page 62

300 acres about 4 miles below mouth of Buckhead Creek bounded
on all sides by vacant land.

****

Odam, Abraham
300 acres in St. George Parish

Surveyed on January 8, 1767   Plat Book C, page 414

300 acres bounded on the southeast by Bryar Creek.

****

Odam, Ephraim
250 acres in St. George Parish

Granted on October 3, 1769   Grant Book G, page 441

250 acres bounded on the northwest by Abraham Lamb.

****

Odam, Frederick
100 acres in St. George Parish

Granted on August 6, 1771   Grant Book I, page 392

100 acres bounded on all sides by vacant land.

****

Odam, Jacob
100 acres in St. George Parish

Granted on May 4, 1773   Grant Book I, page 991

100 acres bounded on all sides by vacant land.

****

Odam, Joshua
100 acres in St. George Parish

Surveyed on January 8, 1761   Plat Book C, page 141
Granted on April 3, 1770   Grant Book G, page 582

100 acres bounded on the northeast by Briar Creek. Surveyed
for Thomas Litch and by order of November 7, 1769, to pass
to Joshua Odam.

****

Odam, Joshua
100 acres in St. George Parish

Granted on April 6, 1773   Grant Book I, page 957

100 acres bounded on all sides by vacant land.

****

O'Daniel, Owen
1000 acres in St. George Parish

Granted on July 5, 1768   Grant Book G, page 139

1000 acres bounded on the northeast by the Savannah River,
southeast and southwest by land ordered Joseph Dunlap.

****

O'Daniel, Owen
150 acres in St. George Parish

Granted on July 5, 1768   Grant Book G, page 140

150 acres bounded on the east by Joseph Perry.

****

Offutt, Archibald
60 acres in St. George Parish

Surveyed on January 15, 1760   Plat Book C, page 415

60 acres bounded on the southeast by land granted John Nelson
and on all other sides by the Savannah River. Original warrant
says that this tract adjoins land granted Benjamin Horn.

****

Ogilby, James
100 acres in St. George Parish

Granted on February 3, 1767   Grant Book F, page 75

100 acres bounded on the northeast by the said James Ogilby.

****

Ogilvie, Peter
100 acres in St. George Parish

Granted on October 6, 1772   Grant Book I, page 773

100 acres bounded on the east by James Ogilvie.

****

Ogleby, James
200 acres in St. George Parish

Surveyed on August 11, 1759   Plat Book C, page 414
Granted on November 2, 1762   Grant Book D, page 237

The original warrant states that the tract was located on
Boggy Gut, a branch of Brier Creek on the path leading from
Savannah to Augusta.

****

Ogleby, James
150 acres in St. George Parish

Granted on April 7, 1767   Grant Book F, page 199

150 acres bounded on all sides by vacant land.

****

160

Oran, Robert
100 acres in St. George Parish

Granted on July 4, 1769   Grant Book G, page 367

100 acres bounded on the east by Abraham Sapp.

****

Orr, Benjamin
100 acres in St. George Parish

Granted on August 4, 1767   Grant Book F, page 320

100 acres bounded on the west by the said Benjamin Orr.

****

Overstreet, Henry
150 acres in St. George Parish

Granted on January 1, 1765   Grant Book E, page 93

150 acres bounded on the northeast by Savannah River, southeast by William Erven and northwest by John Macknie.

****

Overstreet, Henry, Jr.
200 acres in St. George Parish

Granted on August 6, 1765   Grant Book E, page 206

200 acres bounded on all sides by vacant land.

****

Overstreet, Henry, Jr.
43 acres in St. George Parish

Granted on September 2, 1766   Grant Book E, page 368

43 acres bounded on the northeast by the Savannah River, and southwest by land ordered to Andrew McCorrie.

****

Overton, Aaron
200 acres in St. George Parish

Granted on June 7, 1768   Grant Book G, page 124

200 acres bounded on all sides by vacant land.

****

Pace, James
500 acres in St. George Parish

Granted on July 5, 1774   Grant Book M, page 84

500 acres bounded on the south by Bledsoe.

****

Pace, Samuel
100 acres in St. George Parish

Granted on October 4, 1774   Grant Book M, page 590

100 acres bounded on the northwest by George Walker and
southwest by Thomas Fussell.

****

Paner, Michael
150 acres in St. George Parish

Granted on November 6, 1764   Grant Book E, page 70

150 acres bounded on the south by George Stregel and north
by John Tanner.

****

Parkinson, John
100 acres in St. George Parish

Granted on March 1, 1768   Grant Book G, page 59

100 acres bounded on the west by Lamberts Big Creek.

****

Parkinson, John and Quinton Pooler
250 acres in St. George Parish

Original survey date unknown
Resurveyed on August 20, 1828   Plat Book M, pages 113 & 117
Granted on May 5, 1772   Grant Book I, page 602

250 acres bounded on the south by Absolom Wells, west by
Catherine Gray. Resurveyed for the estate of Dr. John
Powell in 1828 and found to contain 308 acres.

****

Pelcher, William
200 acres in St. George Parish

Granted on August 2, 1774   Grant Book M, page 241

200 acres bounded on the southwest by Great Ogechee River.

****

Pendry, William
200 acres in St. George Parish

Granted on July 7, 1767   Grant Book F, page 301

200 acres bounded on the east by Luke Deane.

****

Pennington, Edward
100 acres in St. George Parish

Granted on June 5, 1770   Grant Book I, page 31

100 acres bounded on the east by John Wills.

****

Penny, John
250 acres in St. George Parish

Granted on April 7, 1772   Grant Book I, page 573

250 acres bounded on northwest by William Hendley, northeast
by William Sleather and Humphreys, partly on the southeast by
the said William Sleather and on all other sides vacant.

****

Penson, Aaron
200 acres in St. George Parish

Granted on October 6, 1767   Grant Book F, page 391

200 acres bounded on the east by Hause (?) Kendrick, west by
Peter Wynne, Jr., and southwest by Peter Wynne, Sr.

****

Perry, Isaac
100 acres in St. George Parish

Granted on March 5, 1765   Grant Book E, page 122

100 acres bounded on the northeast by Savannah River, southeast
by William Newberry and west by James McKay.

****

Perry, Isaac
100 acres in St. George Parish

Granted on March 3, 1767   Grant Book F, page 139

100 acres bounded on all sides by vacant land.

****

Perry, Isaac
47 acres in St. George Parish

Granted on March 1, 1768   Grant Book H, page 7

47 acres bounded on the northeast by Savannah River, northwest
by James Mackay and southeast by the said Isaac Perry.

****

Perry, Joseph
100 acres in St. George Parish

Surveyed on May 28, 1759   Plat Book C, page 418
Granted on August 2, 1763   Grant Book D, page 321

100 acres bounded north by the Savannah River. Original warrant
states that tract was located about 25 miles above the mouth
of Brier Creek at a place called Beaver Dam or Joblers Bottom.

****

Pettycrew, John
500 acres in St. George Parish

Surveyed on August 2, 1760   Plat Book C, page 418

500 acres bounded on the northeast by Savannah River, and
northwest by David Douglass. Original warrant states that
tract is located between a place called the Corn House and
King Creek near adjoining 1000 acres granted Lachlan McGillivray.

****

Phillips, John
100 acres in St. George Parish

Granted on October 29, 1765   Grant Book E, page 304

100 acres bounded on all sides by vacant land.

****

Philpot, William
100 acres in St. George Parish

Granted on July 7, 1772   Grant Book I, page 660

100 acres bounded on the northeast by (?) Moxley, southeast
by Bready's land and northwest by (?) Dean.

****

Pier, Robert
200 acres in St. George Parish

Granted on June 5, 1770   Grant Book I, page 30

200 acres bounded on all sides by vacant land.

****

Pierce, Edmund
400 acres in St. George Parish

Granted on October 4, 1768   Grant Book G, page 202

400 acres bounded on all sides by vacant land.

****

Pierce, James
100 acres in St. George Parish

Granted on July 7, 1767   Grant Book F, page 300

100 acres bounded on the southeast by John Williams and on
the northeast by John Royal.

****

Pierce, James
100 acres in St. George Parish

Granted on January 3, 1769   Grant Book G, page 256

100 acres bounded on all sides by vacant land.

****

Pilcher, Edward
150 acres in St. George Parish

Granted on February 7, 1775   Grant Book M, page 1040

150 acres bounded on the west by Ogechee River and southeast
by ------Yarborough.

****

Pilsher, Edward
200 acres in St. George Parish

Granted on April 4, 1769   Grant Book G, page 303

200 acres bounded on the east by a branch of McBeans Swamp.

****

Pilsher, William
100 acres in St. George Parish

Granted on May 7, 1771   Grant Book I, page 317

100 acres bounded on the north by land of William Davis.

****

Plummer, Micajah
150 acres in St. George Parish

Granted on October 29, 1765   Grant Book F, page 375

150 acres bounded on the northeast by Ogechee River, southeast by Martin Dasher and southwest by John Lane.

****

Poll, Catherine
200 acres in St. George Parish

Granted on September 6, 1774   Grant Book M, page 369

200 acres bounded on the southwest by Briar Creek and southeast by John Royal.

****

Pool, Catherine
150 acres in St. George Parish

Granted on January 19, 1773   Grant Book I, page 876

150 acres bounded on the southwest by Brier Creek, southeast by John Thornhill and north by James Gray.

****

Pooler, Quintin
350 acres in St. George Parish

Granted on July 2, 1771   Grant Book I, page 369

350 acres bounded on the southeast by Henry Yonge and northeast by W. Eviston.

****

Pooler, Quintin
150 acres in St. George Parish

Granted on July 2, 1771   Grant Book I, page 370

150 acres bounded on all sides by vacant land.

****

Pooler, Quintin and John Parkinson
250 acres in St. George Parish

Original survey unknown
Resurveyed on August 20, 1828   Plat Book M, pages 113 & 117
Granted on May 5, 1772   Grant Book I, page 602

250 acres bounded on the south by Absolom Wells, west by Catherine
Gray. Resurveyed for the estate of Dr. John Powell in 1828
and found to contain 308 acres.

****

Port, James
300 acres in St. George Parish

Granted on December 6, 1774   Grant Book M, page 820

300 acres bounded on the northeast by Mr. Hescoot.

****

Port, James
300 acres in St. George Parish

Granted on December 6, 1774   Grant Book M, page 821

300 acres bounded on the southwest by Benjamin Horn.

****

Porter, William
200 acres in St. George Parish

Granted on March 5, 1765   Grant Book E, page 118

200 acres bounded on all sides by vacant land.

****

Porter, William
100 acres in St. George Parish

Granted on August 4, 1767   Grant Book F, page 323

100 acres bounded on the southwest by the said William Porter.

****

Powell, John
250 acres in St. George Parish

Granted on October 1, 1771   Grant Book I, page 440

250 acres bounded on all sides by vacant land.

****

Powell, Dr. John
250 acres in St. George Parish

Original survey unknown
Resurveyed on August 20, 1828   Plat Book M, pages 113 & 117
Granted on May 5, 1772   Grant Book I, page 602

250 acres granted to Quintin Pooler and John Parkinson and
bounded on the south by Absolom Wells, west by Catherine
Gray. Resurveyed for the estate of Dr. John Powell in 1828
and found to contain 308 acres.

****

Powell, Lewis
200 acres in St. George Parish

Granted on July 7, 1772   Grant Book I, page 694

200 acres bounded on all sides by vacant land.

****

Powell, William
150 acres in St. George Parish

Granted on August 4, 1767   Grant Book F, page 322

150 acres bounded on the northwest by Josiah Dixon.

****

Preston, Henry
500 acres in St. George Parish

Granted on June 7, 1774   Grant Book I, page 1026

500 acres bounded on southwest by Bryer Creek and northwest
by Captain Read.

****

Prethero, John
300 acres in St. George Parish

Granted on September 30, 1757   Grant Book A, page 460

300 acres in the District of Halifax bounded on the west by
Daniel Shubdrein and northeast by the Savannah River.

****

Prothro, Solomon
150 acres in St. George Parish

Granted on May 3, 1768   Grant Book G, page 106

150 acres bounded on all sides by vacant land.

****

Pugh, Francis
100 acres in St. George Parish

Granted on February 2, 1768   Grant Book G, page 28

100 acres bounded on the northeast by William Ducker.

****

Pugh, Francis
150 acres in St. George Parish

Granted on March 5, 1771   Grant Book I, page 274

150 acres bounded on the southwest by land ordered John Rountree.

****

Pugh, James
200 acres in St. George Parish

Granted on August 6, 1765   Grant Book E, page 208

200 acres bounded on the north by Buckhead Creek, east by Jesse
Wiggins and west by William Ducker.

****

Pugh, James
100 acres in St. George Parish

Granted on October 29, 1765   Grant Book E, page 265

100 acres bounded on all sides by vacant land.

****

Queen, James M.
50 acres in St. George Parish

Granted on January 19, 1773   Grant Book H, page 95

50 acres on bounty bounded on the northwest by land of the said grantee.

****

Rae, Ann
500 acres in St. George Parish

Surveyed on January 3, 1772   Plat Book M, page 44
Granted on March 3, 1772   Grant Book I, page 522

500 acres bounded on the southwest by the Ogechee River.

****

Rae, James, Robert Rae, John Rae, Samuel Elbert, Thomas Graham
391 acres in St. George Parish

Granted on December 6, 1774   Grant Book M, page 824

391 acres bounded on the northwest by land ordered David Cavenah, southeast by unknown land, northeast by vacant land and southwest by the Ogechee River.

****

Rae, James, Robert Rae, John Rae, Samuel Elbert, Thomas Graham
109 acres in St. George Parish

Granted on December 6, 1774   Grant Book M, page 825

109 acres bounded east by John Rae, north by -- Robinson and southwest by Briar Creek.

****

Rae, John
150 acres in St. George Parish

Granted on October 29, 1765   Grant Book E, page 270

150 acres bounded on all sides by vacant land.

****

Rae, John
100 acres in St. George Parish

Granted on June 2, 1767   Grant Book F, page 278

100 acres bounded on all sides by vacant land.

****

Rae, John
100 acres in St. George Parish

Granted on December 1, 1767   Grant Book F, page 426

100 acres bounded on all sides by vacant land.

****

Rae, John
200 acres in St. George Parish

Granted on October 4, 1768   Grant Book G, page 203

200 acres bounded on the northeast by Briar Creek and east
by the said John Rae.

****

Rae, John
200 acres in St. George Parish

Granted on October 3, 1769   Grant Book G, page 442

200 acres bounded on the southeast, southwest and northwest
by the said John Rae.

****

172

Rae, John
300 acres in St. George Parish

Granted on January 7, 1772   Grant Book I, page 501

300 acres bounded partly on the east by land of --- Wilkie,
partly on the west by land of the said grantee, Briar Creek
and north by vacant land.

                              ****

Rae, John, James Rae, Robert Rae, Samuel Elbert, Thomas Graham
391 acres in St. George Parish

Granted on December 6, 1774   Grant Book M, page 824

391 acres bounded by land ordered David Cavenah, southeast by
unknown land, northeast by vacant land and southwest by the
Ogechee River.

                              ****

Rae, John, Robert Rae, James Rae, Samuel Elbert, Graham Thomas
109 acres in St. George Parish

Granted December 6, 1774   Grant Book M, page 825

109 acres bounded on the east by John Rae, north by ___ Robinson,
and southwest by Briar Creek.

                              ****

Rae, John, Robert Rae, Samuel Elbert and Thomas Graham
150 acres in St. George Parish

Granted on November 1, 1774   Grant Book M, page 725

150 acres bounded on the northeast by Edmund Pearce and by
vacant land, southwest by Arthur Wall and on the west by
Isaac Perry.

                              ****

Rae, John, Jr.
200 acres in St. George Parish

Granted on June 2, 1767   Grant Book F, page 279

200 acres bounded on all sides by vacant land.

Rae, Robert, James Rae, John Rae, Samuel Elbert, Thomas Graham
391 acres in St. George Parish

Granted on December 6, 1774   Grant Book M, page 824

391 acres bounded by land ordered David Cavenah, southeast by unknown land, northeast by vacant and southwest by Ogechee River.

****

Rae, Robert, James Rae, John Rae, Samuel Elbert, Thomas Graham
109 acres in St. George Parish

Granted on December 6, 1774   Grant Book M, page 825

109 acres bounded on the east by John Rae, north by ---Robinson and southwest by Briar Creek.

****

Rae, Robert, John Rae, Samuel Elbert and Tomas Graham
150 acres in St. George Parish

Granted on November 1, 1774   Grant Book M, page 725

150 acres bounded on the northeast by Edmund Pearce and vacant land, southwest by Arthur Wall and west by Isaac Perry.

****

Rains, William
150 acres in St. George Parish

Granted on May 1, 1759   Grant Book B, page 164

150 acres bounded on all sides by vacant land.

****

Randon, Peter
350 acres in St. George Parish

Surveyed on May 27, 1761   Plat Book C, page 419
Granted on May 21, 1762   Grant Book D, page 129

350 acres bounded on the southeast by James Nesmith, northeast by the Savannah River and northwest by Peter Randon. Surveyed as Randol. (Original warrant on file).

****

Randon, Peter
200 acres in St. George Parish

Granted on February 1, 1763   Grant Book D, page 282

200 acres bounded on the northeast by the said Peter Randon.

****

Read, James
600 acres in St. George Parish

Granted on July 7, 1772   Grant Book I, page 671

600 acres bounded on all sides by vacant land.

****

Read, James
400 acres in St. George Parish

Granted on July 7, 1772   Grant Book I, page 693

400 acres bounded on the northwest by --- Derioe, south by
---Jorden and Joel Walker and east by James Castilow.

****

Read, James
500 acres in St. George Parish

Granted on July 5, 1774   Grant Book M, page 96

500 acres bounded on the southwest by Bryer Creek.

****

Read, James
500 acres in St. George Parish

Granted on December 6, 1774   Grant Book M, page 826

500 acres bounded on the east by land ordered to Samuel
Harris.

****

Read, James
500 acres in St. George Parish

Granted on December 6, 1774   Grant Book M, page 827

500 acres bounded on the southwest by vacant land and one
Warnocks, northeast by vacant land and Gideon Thomas.

****

Read, James and James DeVaux, in trust for William Handley
500 acres in St. George Parish

Granted on July 5, 1774   Grant Book M, page 98

500 acres bounded on the northwest by Nunes and John Lott.

****

Read, James, James DeVaux, in trust for William Handley
500 acres in St. George Parish

Original survey date unknown
Resurveyed on May 19, 1829   Plat Book M, page 124
Granted on July 5, 1774   Grant Book M, page 97

500 acres bounded on the south by ---Pray, west by Helvenstine,
and east by Bledsoe. Resurveyed in 1829 for Joshua Clebborn
and found to contain 378 acres.

****

Read, William
100 acres in St. George Parish

Granted on September 6, 1774   Grant Book M, page 401

100 acres bounded on the northeast and southeast by Emanuel,
south by James Fleming and southwest by John McCanlis, and
all being in the Queensborough Township, and also Town Lot
67 in Queensborough.

****

Red, James
94 acres in St. George Parish

Granted on October 31, 1765   Grant Book E, page 277

94 acres bounded on the east by the Savannah River, northwest by Alexander Wood and southwest by Thomas Red.

****

Red, Reuben
100 acres in St. George Parish

Granted on June 6, 1769   Grant Book G, page 344

100 acres bounded on the southeast by John Fryer and northeast by Thomas Red.

****

Red, Thomas
300 acres in St. George Parish

Surveyed on April 13, 1758   Plat Book M, page 112
Granted on October 2, 1759   Grant Book B, page 443

300 acres bounded on the west by Benjamin Williamson and northeast by the Savannah River.

****

Red, Thomas
764 acres in St. George Parish

Granted on October 31, 1765   Grant Book E, page 276

764 acres bounded on the east by Alexander Wood and the Savannah River, south by John Fryer, northwest by Samuel Alexander, Benjamin Horn, William Session and Thomas Red.

****

Red, Thomas
150 acres in St. George Parish

Granted on July 7, 1767   Grant Book F, page 304

150 acres bounded on all sides by vacant land.

****

Red, Thomas
100 acres in St. George Parish

Granted on January 2, 1770   Grant Book G, page 505

100 acres bounded on all sides by vacant land.

****

Redding, William
250 acres in St. George Parish

Granted on October 4, 1774   Grant Book M, page 593

250 acres bounded on the east by ----McDaniel and north
by ----Mabley.

****

Reeves, John
250 acres in St. George Parish

Granted on August 4, 1767   Grant Book F, page 325

250 acres bounded on all sides by vacant land.

****

Rel, Paul Haroldson
200 acres in St. George Parish

Granted on April 13, 1761   Grant Book C, page 69

200 acres bounded on all sides by vacant land.

****

Rhodes, William
200 acres in St. George Parish

Granted on April 2, 1765   Grant Book E, page 133

200 acres located 92 miles from Savannah, bounded on the
northwest by the Savannah River, southwest by Andrew Griner,
southeast by John Longe and a great lake and northeast by
James Gray.

****

Richardson, Benjamin
200 acres in St. George Parish

Granted on August 2, 1774   Grant Book M, page 245

200 acres bounded on the northeast by Dukes Pond and vacant
land.

****

Ring, Christopher and Peter Blyth
400 acres in St. George Parish

Granted on October 2, 1764   Grant Book E, page 49

400 acres on Rocky Creek originally surveyed for Charles
Gee, but granted to Ring and Blyth as creditors of Gee.

****

Rivers, Thomas
100 acres in St. George Parish

Granted on October 4, 1774   Grant Book M, page 595

100 acres bounded on the west by John Fitch.

****

Roberts, Eisom
200 acres in St. George Parish

Granted on August 6, 1765   Grant Book E, page 209

200 acres bounded on the southwest by the Great Ogechee River.

****

Roberts, James
82 acres in St. George Parish

Granted on March 3, 1767   Grant Book F, page 142

82 acres bounded on the east by the Savannah River, south by the
said river and land of David Hughes, north by Nicholas Fisher
and west by the said James Roberts.

****

Roberts, James
150 acres in St. George Parish

Granted on September 1, 1767   Grant Book F, page 365

150 acres bounded on the north by William Colson, east by
Nehemiah Tindall and south by John Gasper Hirtschman.

****

Roberts, James
100 acres in St. George Parish

Granted on January 5, 1773   Grant Book I, page 835

100 acres bounded on all sides by vacant land.

****

Roberts, John
350 acres in St. George Parish

Granted on June 2, 1767   Grant Book F, page 280

350 acres bounded on the north by John Tanner and on the
south by James Anderson.

****

Roberts, John
200 acres in St. George Parish

Surveyed on July 14, 1769   Plat Book M, page 20
Granted on October 6, 1772   Grant Book I, page 751

200 acres bounded on the northwest and partly on the northeast by Richard Womack and on all other sides by vacant land.

****

Roberts, Josiah
200 acres in St. George Parish

Granted on April 4, 1769   Grant Book G, page 304

200 acres bounded on the southeast by William Downey.

****

Roberts, Josiah
150 acres in St. George Parish

Granted on June 5, 1771   Grant Book I, page 349

150 acres bounded on the southeast by land of the said grantee.

****

Robinson, James
200 acres in St. George Parish

Granted on September 6, 1774   Grant Book M, page 395

200 acres in the Township of Queensborough and bounded on all sides by vacant land.

****

Robson, Clotworthy
100 acres in St. George Parish

Granted on July 3, 1770   Grant Book I, page 107

100 acres in the Township of Queensborough bounded on the northeast by Lambeths Big Creek, south by William Harding, west by the Town Common and north by Patrick McKay, and also Town Lot 11 in the Town of Queensborough.

****

Roche, Matthew
1000 acres in St. George Parish

Granted on February 7, 1764   Grant Book D, page 375

1000 acres bounded on the south by Briar Creek, northeast by the Savannah River, north by John Pettycrew and west by Andrew McCurry.

****

Rodgers, James
200 acres in St. George Parish

Granted on September 6, 1774   Grant Book M, page 403

200 acres in Township of Queensborough bounded on all sides by vacant land and also lot 43 in the Town of Queensborough.

****

Rogers, John
150 acres in St. George Parish

Granted on January 3, 1775   Grant Book M, page 934

150 acres bounded on the southeast by William Bland.

****

Rogers, Robert
450 acres in St. George Parish

Granted on September 6, 1774   Grant Book M, page 398

450 acres in Queensborough Township, bounded on the south
by Daniel McNeal and John Brown and north and east by
Samuel Fleming, and also Town Lot 44 in the Town of
Queensborough.

****

Rogers, Robert
100 acres in St. George Parish

Granted on September 6, 1774   Grant Book M, page 399

100 acres bounded on all sides by vacant land.

****

Ross, Hugh
300 acres in St. George Parish

Surveyed on September 22, 1761   Plat Book C, page 419
Granted on May 21, 1762   Grant Book D, page 94

300 acres in Halifax District near lands granted Joshua Atkinson.

****

Ross, Hugh
350 acres in St. George Parish

Granted on November 7, 1769   Grant Book G, page 465

350 acres bounded on the northwest by James Grant and on the
southeast by William Burney.

****

Roundtree, William
300 acres in St. George Parish

Granted on October 6, 1772   Grant Book I, page 754

300 acres bounded on the west by ---Roundtree and east by ---Bass

****

Rountree, Jethro
600 acres in St. George Parish

Granted on October 29, 1765   Grant Book E, page 302

600 acres bounded on the north side of the Great Ogechee
River at a place called Bark Camp.

****

Royal, John
200 acres in St. George Parish

Surveyed on January 9, 1760   Plat Book C, page 419
Granted on November 6, 1764   Grant Book E, page 67

200 acres bounded on the north by the Savannah River. The
original warrant states that the tract is in Halifax District
near land granted Thomas Bell.

****

Royal, Smauel
200 acres in St. George Parish

Surveyed on February 22, 1761   Plat Book C, page 419
Granted on November 6, 1764   Grant Book E, page 68

200 acres bounded on the northwest by Samuel Harne, east by
John Royal, southwest by a lake and south by Thomas Bell
and William Cotherer. The plat of survey shows that on the
south the land was that of Thomas Bibb instead of Thomas
Bell. The original warrant states that the tract is located
in Halifax District, about twenty miles above Briar Creek
at a place called the Great Sweetwater, to run between a
known path there and the Savannah River.

****

Russell, David
50 acres in St. George Parish

Granted on August 2, 1774   Grant Book H, page 116

50 acres in the Township of Queensborough bounded partly on
the east by land of the said grantee, partly on the west
by land of ---Cherry and on all other sides by vacant land.

****

Russell, David
400 acres in St. George Parish

Granted on July 3, 1770   Grant Book I, page 108

400 acres in the Township of Queensborough and bounded on
the southwest by Rocky Comfort Creek.

****

Ryal, John
200 acres in St. George Parish

Granted on May 5, 1772   Grant Book I, page 603

200 acres bounded on the southeast by Moses Mulkey and on
the southwest by Brier Creek.

****

Sallers, Thomas
100 acres in St. George Parish

Granted on May 4, 1773   Grant Book I, page 995

100 acres bounded on the northwest by George Galphin, southwest by John Sellers and southeast by Nicholas Cavena.

****

Sampson, Robert
86 acres in St. George Parish

Granted on January 3, 1775   Grant Book M, page 938

86 acres in Queensborough Township, bounded on the north by Samuel Gibson, John Morrison and Samuel Clements, west by John Ingram and Adam Mickleroy and southeast by Black Jack Branch and land of William Little.

****

Sampson, William
150 acres in St. George Parish

Surveyed on February 20, 1771   Plat Book C, page 348
Granted on April 6, 1773   Grant Book I, page 958

150 acres in the Township of Queensborough bounded on the east by Robert Brison, northwest by John Kennedy and south by Robert Dumville and Crossley, and also Town Lot 24 in the Town of Queensborough.

****

Sanders, Joseph
400 acres in St. George Parish

Surveyed on June 8, 1769   Plat Book C, page 326
Granted on July 3, 1770   Grant Book I, page 109

400 acres in the Township of Queensborough bounded on the south by Matthew Moore, west by Reedy Branch, partly on the east by Robert Girvin and partly by James Hadin, and partly on the north by Matthew Lysle and partly by land vacant, and also Town Lot 17 in the Town of Queensborough. The plat of survey shows that the tract is bounded on the west by Reedy Branch and Thomas Bailey, James Thompson and John Bartholowmew.

****

Sanders, Willima
250 acres in St. George Parish

Granted on August 2, 1774   Grant Book M, page 259

250 acres bounded on the northeast by Briar Creek.

****

Sapp, Abraham
100 acres in St. George Parish

Granted on September 3, 1765   Grant Book E, page 239

100 acres bounded on the east by Briar Creek, north by Elijah Sapp, south by Anthony Brunnell and west by vacant land.

****

Sapp, Abraham
150 acres in St. George Parish

Granted on June 2, 1767   Grant Book F, page 281

150 acres bounded on the northeast by Edward Barnard.

****

Sapp, Elijah
100 acres in St. George Parish

Granted on September 3, 1765   Grant Book E, page 238

100 acres bounded on the northeast by Briar Creek, south by Abraham Sapp and west by vacant lands.

****

Sapp, Elijah
100 acres in St. George Parish

Surveyed on May 6, 1769   Plat Book C, page 334
Granted on August 1, 1769   Grant Book G, page 398

100 acres bounded on the southeast by John Mann.

****

Sapp, Elijah
100 acres in St. George Parish

Granted on November 1, 1774   Grant Book M, page 737

100 acres bounded on the north by William Sapp and on the east by Henry Sapp.

****

Sapp, Henry
300 acres in St. Matthew and St. George Parish

Granted on December 2, 1766   Grant Book E, page 408

300 acres bounded on all sides by vacant land.

****

Sapp, Jesse
100 acres in St. George Parish

Surveyed on May 28, 1770   Plat Book C, page 321

100 acres bounded on all sides by vacant land.

****

Sapp, John
150 acres in St. George Parish

Surveyed on October 26, 1765   Plat Book C, page 307
Granted on July 7, 1767   Grant Book F, page 305

150 acres bounded on all sides by vacant land.

****

Sapp, John
200 acres in St. George Parish

Granted on May 4, 1773   Grant Book I, page 994

200 acres bounded on the west by William Sapp, partly on the south and partly east by Henry Sapp and on all other sides by vacant land.

****

Sapp, William
200 acres in St. George Parish

Granted on September 2, 1766   Grant Book E, page 371

200 acres bounded on the north by Briar Creek.

****

Sapp, William
100 acres in St. George Parish

187

Surveyed on December 1, 1769   Plat Book C, page 314
Granted on September 6, 1774   Grant Book M, page 408

100 acres bounded on all sides by vacant land.

****

Savage, Robert
150 acres in St. George Parish

Granted on September 1, 1767   Grant Book F, page 367

150 acres bounded on all sides by vacant land.

****

Savage, Thomas
500 acres in St. George Parish

Surveyed on October 13, 1772   Plat Book C, page 356
Granted on July 5, 1774   Grant Book M, page 111

500 acres bounded on the east by George Galphin and ---
Helvenstine, west by the said Thomas Savage and ____
Castlelow and north by surveyed land.

****

Savage, Thomas
500 acres in St. George Parish

Surveyed on October 14, 1772   Plat Book C, page 351
Granted on July 5, 1774   Grant Book M, page 112

500 acres bounded on the west by ----Derisoro, south by
----Castillow and east by the said Thomas Savage.

****

Scott, John
350 acres in St. George Parish

Granted on October 4, 1774   Grant Book M, page 601

350 acres bounded on the southeast by a branch and land of
John Howell and southwest by ----Garvey.

****

Scruggs, Richard
300 acres in St. George Parish

Surveyed on December 15, 1757   Plat Book C, page 423

300 acres bounded on the northwest by Huston and northeast by Bryer Creek.

****

Scruggs, Richard
350 acres in St. George Parish

Surveyed on November 13, 1762   Plat Book C, page 338

350 acres originally surveyed for Scruggs, thence ordered to Thomas Irwin on October 2, 1764, and bounded north and east by the Savannah River, north by Nehemiah Tindall and south by Robert Bevil.

****

Seaburn, Edward
150 acres in St. George Parish

Surveyed on May 20, 1772   Plat Book C, page 423

150 acres bounded on the northeast by Moses Cressup, southeast by Charles Gee and southwest by William Downey and vacant land.

****

Sellers, John
350 acres in St. George Parish

Granted on April 5, 1768   Grant Book G, page 86

350 acres bounded on the north by George Galphin, northeast by land ordered the said John Sellers and on the southeast partly by Henry Cavenah.

****

Sellers, John
100 acres in St. George Parish

Surveyed on January 30, 1767   Plat Book C, page 313

100 acres originally surveyed for John Sellers, thence ordered to Charles Cavenah on February 5, 1771.

****

Shand, Peter
100 acres in St. George Parish

Surveyed on October 30, 1767   Plat Book C, page 300
Granted on May 3, 1768   Grant Book G, page 109

100 acres bounded on the northeast by Samuel Wilkey and northwest by James Gray. Plat shows that the tract is bounded on the northwest by James Way instead of Gray.

****

Sharp, Henry
250 acres in St. George Parish

Surveyed on December 30, 1767   Plat Book C, page 324

250 acres bounded on the northwest by Isham Roberts and southwest by the Ogechee River and vacant land.

****

Sharp, John
300 acres in St. George Parish

Surveyed on August 15, 1769   Plat Book C, page 311
Granted on February 4, 1772   Grant Book I, page 520

300 acres bounded on the southeast by David Lewis.

****

Sharp, Lydia
400 acres in St. George Parish

Granted on October 6, 1767   Grant Book F, page 394

400 acres bounded on the northeast by John Sharp, southeast and southwest by James Murphee.

****

Sheffield, William
200 acres in St. George Parish

Granted on January 3, 1775   Grant Book M, page 939

200 acres bounded on all sides by vacant land.

****

Sheftall, Benjamin and Sheftall Sheftall
150 acres in St. George Parish

Granted on July 5, 1774   Grant Book M, page 105

150 acres bounded on the northwest by ----McCurrie and southeast by land supposed to be granted to some person unknown.

****

Sheftall, Levi and Mordecai Sheftall
400 acres in St. George Parish

Surveyed on October 16, 1765   Plat Book C, page 142
Granted on June 7, 1768   Grant Book G, page 126

400 acres surveyed for Andrew Lambert, thence ordered on
February 2, 1768 to Mordecai and Levi Sheftall.

****

Sheftall, Levi and Mordecai Sheftall
200 acres in St. George Parish

Surveyed on October 16, 1765   Plat Book C, page 142
Granted on June 7, 1768   Grant Book G, page 127

200 acres surveyed for Andrew Lambert and thence ordered to
Mordecai and Levi Sheftall.

****

Sheftall, Mordecai
1000 acres in St. George Parish

Granted on August 4, 1767   Grant Book F, page 333

1000 acres bounded on the north by ----Friar, widow, and Francis Stringer, northeast by the Savannah River and east by Stephen Smith.

****

Sheftall, Mordecai
300 acres in St. George Parish

Granted on July 5, 1774   Grant Book M, page 107

300 acres bounded on the southeast by John Graham, southwest by Thomas Frederick and west by Briar Creek.

****

Sheftall, Mordecai
300 acres in St. George Parish

Granted on January 3, 1775   Grant Book M, page 942

300 acres bounded on the southeast by Thomas Sherman and southwest by the Ogechee River.

****

Sheftall, Mordecai and Levi Shedtall
400 acres in St. George Parish

Surveyed on October 16, 1765   Plat Book C, page 142
Granted on June 7, 1768   Grant Book G, page 126

400 acres surveyed for Andrew Lambert, thence ordered on February 2, 1768 to Mordecai and Levi Sheftall.

****

Sheftall, Mordecai and Levi Sheftall
200 acres in St. George Parish

Surveyed on October 16, 1765   Plat Book C, page 142
Granted on June 7, 1768   Grant Book G, page 127

200 acres surveyed for Andrew Lambert, thence ordered to Mordecai and Levi Sheftall.

****

Sheftall, Shedtall and Benjamin Sheftall
150 acres in St. George Parish

Granted on July 5, 1774   Grant Book M, page 105

150 acres bounded on the northwest by ----McCurrie and southeast by land supposed to be granted to some person unknown.

****

Shelly, William
200 acres in St. George Parish

Granted on July 5, 1774   Grant Book M, page 118

200 acres in the Township of Queensborough and bounded on
all sides by vacant land.

****

Shephard, Richard
100 acres in St. George Parish

Surveyed on June 15, 1772   Plat Book C, page 358
Granted on October 6, 1772   Grant Book I, page 757

100 acres bounded on the southeast by Frances Robes, north
by Thomas Ford and Emanuel and west by ----Emanuel. Surveyed
as Shepherd and granted as Shephard.

****

Sherbert, James
100 acres in St. George Parish

Granted on March 2, 1773   Grant Book I, page 922

100 acres bounded on the west by Elias Miller and east by
----Bryan.

****

Sherman, Thomas
200 acres in St. George Parish

Granted on December 6, 1774   Grant Book M, page 828

200 acres bounded on the northwest by Mordecai Sheftall and
southwest by the Ogechee River.

Shirley, William
250 acres in St. Paul and St. George Parishes

Granted on November 7, 1769   Grant Book G, page 466

250 acres bounded on all sides by vacant land.

****

Shirley, William
200 acres in St. George Parish

Granted on October 6, 1772   Grant Book I, page 777

200 acres bounded on all sides by vacant land.

****

Shruder, Thomas
100 acres in St. George Parish

Granted on May 4, 1773   Grant Book I, page 996

100 acres bounded on the northeast by the Savannah River and northwest by Jonathon Mulkey.

****

Shruder, Thomas
150 acres in St. George Parish

Granted on August 2, 1774   Grant Book M, page 248

150 acres bounded on the northwest by the Savannah River and southwest in part by land of James Gray.

****

Shruder, Thomas
250 acres in St. George Parish

Granted on August 2, 1774   Grant Book M, page 250

250 acres bounded on all sides by vacant land.

****

Shruder, Thomas
500 acres in St. George Parish

Granted on August 2, 1774   Grant Book M, page 251

500 acres bounded on the southwest by Briar Creek and northwest by land surveyed for John McQueen.

****

Simpson, James
200 acres in St. George Parish

Surveyed on February 22, 1771   Plat Book C, page 332
Granted on June 5, 1771   Grant Book I, page 351

200 acres bounded on all sides by vacant land.

****

Simpson, John
1000 acres in St. George Parish

Granted on October 4, 1774   Grant Book M, page 596

1000 acres bounded on the northwest by William Newberry and
northeast by Thomas Red.

****

Sims, Thomas
100 acres in St. George Parish

Granted on March 3, 1767   Grant Book F, page 145

100 acres bounded on the northwest by William Adams.

****

Sims, Thomas
100 acres in St. George Parish

Surveyed on April 14, 1769   Plat Book C, page 299
Granted on July 4, 1769   Grant Book G, page 370

100 acres bounded on all sides by vacant land.

****

Sims, Thomas
100 acres in St. George Parish

Surveyed on January 9, 1769   Plat Book C, page 316
Granted on August 1, 1769   Grant Book G, page 399

The plat of survey shows that this tract was bounded on the
north by Brier Creek.

****

Singleton, Philip
200 acres in St. George Parish

Surveyed on February 25, 1772   Plat Book C, page 355
Granted on October 6, 1772   Grant Book I, page 753

200 acres surveyed as Philip Shingleton.

****

Singleton, Philip
250 acres in St. George Parish

Surveyed on September 23, 1768   Plat Book C, page 312

250 acres bounded on the southeast by Rancol Bracy.

****

Sisson, Thomas
150 acres in St. George Parish

Surveyed on November 14, 1758   Plat Book M, page 112
Granted on February 5, 1760   Grant Book B, page 382

150 acres bounded on the north by the Savannah River and
west by Thomas Red.

****

Sissin, William
150 acres in St. George Parish

Surveyed on August 15, 1759   Plat Book C, page 297 & 424
Granted on July 2, 1765   Grant Book E, page 183

150 acres originally surveyed for William Sissin and thence "regranted to John Fryer by order of October 2, 1764, and located 104 miles from Savannah, bounded on the northeast by the Savannah River. Original warrant states that the tract is located at the head of the Long Reaches about 6 miles below Withringtons Bluff by land, in Halifax District, in lieu of 150 acres granted him on an island opposite Tuckaseekings.

****

Sizemore, Edward
150 acres in St. George Parish

Surveyed on March 29, 1764   Plat Book M, page 66
Granted on August 6, 1765   Grant Book E, page 214

150 acres bounded on the east by Robert Heaton.

****

Skelly, William
100 acres in St. George Parish

Granted on July 3, 1770   Grant Book I, page 111

100 acres in the Township of Queensborough bounded on the east by Lambeths Creek and south by Robert Girvin, and also Town Lot 48 in the Town of Queensborough.

****

Skelly, William
250 acres in St. George Parish

Surveyed on February 14, 1771   Plat Book C, page 346

250 acres in St. George Parish bounded on all sides by vacant land.

****

Skinner, William
100 acres in St. George

Surveyed on July 14, 1770   Plat Book C, page 309

100 acres bounded on the southwest by Doharts Creek.

****

Slocumb, Seth
100 acres in St. George Parish

Surveyed on February 15, 1769   Plat Book C, page 304
Granted on May 7, 1771   Grant Book I, page 318

100 acres bounded on all sides by vacant land.

****

Slocumb, Seth
100 acres in St. George Parish

Granted on September 6, 1774   Grant Book M, page 414

100 acres bounded on the southwest by Robert Pyor.

****

Smith, John
50 acres in St. George Parish

Surveyed on October 23, 1770   Plat Book C, page 344
Granted on February 4, 1772   Grant Book H, page 70

50 acres bounded on the southeast by land of the said grantee.

****

Smith, John
200 acres in St. George Parish

Surveyed on October 24, 1770   Plat Book C, page 344
Granted on May 7, 1771   Grant Book I, page 323

200 acres bounded on the northwest by William Jones.

****

Smith, John
100 acres in St. George Parish

Surveyed on March 25, 1771   Plat Book C, page 340
Granted on February 4, 1772   Grant Book I, page 517

100 acres bounded on the southwest by Fitzgerald, northwest by
Ducker, northeast by the said grantee. Plat shows Dukes Pond.

****

Smith, John
100 acres in St. George Parish

Granted on February 4, 1772   Grant Book I, page 518

100 acres bounded on the southwest by land of the said Grantee.

****

Smith, John
200 acres in St. George Parish

Surveyed on October 18, 1768   Plat Book C, page 295
Granted on February 4, 1772   Grant Book I, page 519

200 acres bounded in part on the southwest by William Young
and part by William Connell, northwest by George Wyche, part
on the northeast by the said grantee and on all other sides
by vacant land.

****

Smith, Robert
200 acres in St. Matthew and St. George Parishes

Granted on August 2, 1774   Grant Book M, page 253

200 acres bounded on all sides by vacant land.

****

Smith, Robert
100 acres in St. George Parish

Granted on August 2, 1774   Grant Book M, page 254

100 acres bounded on the northeast by Briar Creek, northwest
by John Rae and southeast by Thomas Sims.

****

Smith, Samuel
100 acres in St. George Parish

Surveyed on February 18, 1772   Plat Book

100 acres in Queensborough Township bounded on the northwest
by James Hamilton and northeast by D. Merren.
****

Smith, Stephen
100 acres in St. George Parish

Granted on October 29, 1765   Grant Book E, page 385

100 acres bounded on the northeast by the Savannah River.

****

Smith, Stephen
300 acres in St. George Parish

Surveyed on June 2, 1770   Plat Book C, page 345
Granted on January 19, 1773   Grant Book I, page 890

300 acres bounded on the northeast by Owen O'Daniel, southeast by Joseph Dunlap and southwest by the said grantee. Plat
shows the tract bounded on the northeast by James Wilson,
southeast and southwest by Joseph Dunlap and northwest by
Owen O'Daniel .

****

Somerall, Henry
100 acres in St. George Parish

Surveyed on September 24, 1761   Plat Book C, page 424
Granted on January 1, 1765   Grant Book E, page 98

100 acres bounded on the south by James Nesmith. The original
warrant states that the tract is located in Halifax District
adjoining John Nesmith and John Mainer.

****

Spires, George
300 acres in St. George Parish

Surveyed December 13, 1770   Plat Book C, page 347
Granted on September 6, 1774   Grant Book M, page 410

300 acres in the Township of Queensborough bounded on the
south by Walter Stephenson.

****

Stanaland, John
200 acres in St. George Parish

Granted on September 6, 1774   Grant Book M, page 411

200 acres bounded on the east by Adam Nesler and north by
William McDonald.

****

Steadhand, Benjamin
100 acres in St. George Parish

Granted on December 3, 1760   Grant Book C, page 9

100 acres bounded on the north by the Savannah River, east
by Thomas Cochran and west by Lattimore Ross.

****

Stedler, Peter
200 acres in St. George Parish

Granted on July 4, 1769   Grant Book G, page 371

200 acres bounded on the northeast by John Conyers and
southeast by the said Peter Stedler.

****

Steedler, Sythe
100 acres in St. George Parish

Surveyed on October 24, 1774   Plat Book M, page 52
Granted on January 3, 1775   Grant Book M, page 937

100 acres bounded on the northeast by land surveyed for
unknown person and southeast by ----Thomas.

****

Stevenson, Walter
200 acres in St. George Parish

Surveyed on June 16, 1769   Plat Book C, page 310
Granted on July 3, 1770   Grant Book I, page 110

201

200 acres in the Township of Queensborough bounded on the south by John Ingram and also Town Lot 34 in the Town of Queensborough.

****

Stewart, David
100 acres in St. George Parish

Surveyed on March 20, 1770   Plat Book C, page 341

100 acres bounded on the northeast by David Wood and Isaac Wood and southwest by Joseph Marshal.

****

Stewart, Peter
150 acres in St. George Parish

Surveyed on October 20, 1770   Plat Book C, page 348
Granted on October 4, 1774   Grant Book M, page 606

150 acres bounded on all sides by vacant land.

****

Stiggins, John
100 acres in St. George Parish

Surveyed on November 22, 1766   Plat Book C, page 309

100 acres bounded on the east by Simon Beekam, south by Briar Creek and north by a path.

****

Stiner, Christian
400 acres in St. George Parish

Surveyed on November 29, 1771   Plat Book C, page 352
Granted on June 2, 1772   Grant Book I, page 636

400 acres bounded on all sides by vacant land.

****

Stiner, David
300 acres in St. George Parish

Granted on June 2, 1772   Grant Book I, page 648

300 acres bounded on the northeast by ----Crumb.

****

Stirk, John
700 acres in St. George Parish

Surveyed on November 9, 1774   Plat Book M, page 48
Granted on March 7, 1775   Grant Book M, page 1089

700 acres bounded on the southwest by the Great Ogechee River, southeast by Philip Mulkey and northwest by land surveyed for Charles Watson.

****

Stirk, John
500 acres in St. George Parish

Surveyed on August 28, 1770   Plat Book C, page 348

500 acres bounded on the northwest by John Graham and on the northeast by Brier Creek.

****

Stokes, Anthony
850 acres in St. George Parish

Surveyed on April 17, 1770   Plat Book C, page 309
Granted on October 2, 1770   Grant Book I, page 176

850 acres bounded on the southwest by James Lambeth and Hugh Ross.

****

Stokes, Anthony
650 acres in St. George Parish

Surveyed on January 31, 1771   Plat Book C, page 347
Granted on May 7, 1771   Grant Book I, page 319

650 acres bounded on all sides by vacant land.

****

Stokes, Anthony
300 acres in St. George Parish

Surveyed on January 31, 1771   Plat Book C, page 344
Granted on May 7, 1771   Grant Book I, page 320

300 acres bounded on all sides by vacant land.

                            ****

Stokes, Anthony
500 acres in St. George Parish

Granted on August 2, 1774   Grant Book M, page 257

500 acres bounded on the west by John Moore.

                            ****

Storr, John
200 acres in St. George Parish

Granted on July 5, 1774   Grant Book M, page 104

200 acres bounded on the southeast by Peter Randon.

                            ****

Stratton, John
100 acres in St. George Parish

Surveyed on March 16, 1765   Plat Book M, page 24
Granted on October 29, 1765   Grant Book E, page 272

100 acres bounded on the northeast by Buckhead Creek and on
the southeast by ----Cavenah.

                            ****

Street, John
200 acres in St. George Parish

Granted on November 3, 1767   Grant Book F, page 413

200 acres bounded on the northeast by Savannah River, south by
Briar Creek and northwest by Matthew Roche.

                            ****

Striegal, George
250 acres in St. George Parish

Surveyed on October 22, 1762   Plat Book C, page 324
Granted on February 3, 1767   Grant Book F, page 78

250 acres bounded on the east by the Savannah River, north
by Michael Peoner and Abraham Lunday, south by Nicholas
Fisher and surveyed as 200 acres.

****

Strigell, George
200 acres St. George Parish

Surveyed on August 10, 1762   Plat Book C, page 296

200 acres bounded on the northwest by the Savannah River,
northeast by Nicholas Fisher, southwest by Michael Pener and
vacant land.

****

Stringer, Francis
200 acres in St. George Parish

Granted on April 2, 1765   Grant Book E, page 132

200 acres located on creeks and branches leading from Reds
Mill.

****

Stringer, Francis
100 acres in St. George Parish

Granted on August 5, 1766   Grant Book E, page 345

100 acres bounded on the east by the Savannah River, north
by John Greyer and south by the said Francis Stringer.

****

Stringer, Francis
200 acres in St. George Parish

Surveyed on February 9, 1773   Plat Book C, page 358
Granted on October 4, 1774   Grant Book M, page 602

200 acres bounded on the west by Simon Bickham, east by Richard----, south by Briar Creek. Plat shows the tract bounded on the east by Richard Cureton.

****

Stringer, Francis
200 acres in St. George Parish

Surveyed on June 1, 1770   Plat Book C, page 338
Granted on August 6, 1771   Grant Book I, page 385

200 acres originally surveyed for Francis Stringer, then ordered to Lemuel Lanier on June 5, 1771. Granted to Lemuel Lanier and bounded on the northeast by the Savannah River, southeast by John Frazer, north by Peter Torquintz, northwest by vacant land and partly on the southwest by Mordecai Sheftall and partly by vacant land.

****

Stuart, Lieutenant Patrick
500 acres in St. George Parish

Granted on October 4, 1774   Grant Bpok M, page 597

500 acres bounded on the southwest by Briar Creek and northwest and southwest by land surveyed for John McLean.

****

Stuart, Lieutenant Patrick
500 acres in St. George Parish

Granted on October 4, 1774   Grant Book M, page 598

500 acres bounded on the southwest by Briar Creek and southeast by land surveyed for John McQueen.

****

Stuart, Patrick
500 acres in St. George Parish

Granted on November 1, 1774   Grant Book M, page 731

500 acres bounded on the north by Captain Stuart adn southwest by the Ogechee River.

****

206

Stuart, Patrick
500 acres in St. George Parish

Granted on November 1, 1774   Grant Book M, page 732

500 acres bounded on all sides by vacant land.

****

Stuart, Patrick
500 acres in St. George Parish

Granted on November 1, 1774   Grant Book M, page 733

500 acres bounded on the southeast by Captain Stuart and
southwest by the Ogechee River.

****

Talley, John
500 acres in St. George Parish

Granted on March 5, 1765   Grant Book E, page 117

500 acres bounded on the east by the Savannah River and
north by David Douglas.

****

Tanehill, John
200 acres in St. George Parish

Granted on April 7, 1767   Grant Book F, page 207

200 acres bounded on the south by Bryar Creek.

****

Tanner, John
150 acres in St. George Parish

Surveyed on May 25, 1765   Plat Book C, page 367
Granted on May 5, 1767   Grant Book F, page 254

150 acres bounded on all sides by vacant land.

****

Tanner, John
100 acres in St. George Parish

Granted on October 6, 1767   Grant Book F, page 395

100 acres on Rocky Creek bounded on the south by John Tanner.

****

Tanner, John
100 acres in St. George Parish

Granted on September 6, 1774   Grant Book M, page 372

100 acres bounded on the northeast by John Tanner and south
by John Roberts.

****

Tarver, Thomas
100 acres in St. George Parish

Granted on January 3, 1775   Grant Book M, page 948

100 acres bounded on all sides by vacant land.

****

Tatnell, Josiah
500 acres partly in St. Matthew and partly in St. George Parish

Granted on April 7, 1767   Grant Book F, page 208

500 acres bounded on the south partly by John Conyers and
partly by Catherine Mullryne and on every other side by
vacant land.

****

Tattnell, Josiah
500 acres in St. George Parish

Granted on September 6, 1774   Grant Book M, page 377

500 acres bounded on the north by land surveyed for said
Josiah Tattnell.

****

Tattnell, Josiah
500 acres in St. George Parish

Granted on September 6, 1774   Grant Book M, page 378

500 acres bounded on the north by ---- Underwood and south
by Josiah Tattnell.

****

Taylor, Jacob
200 acres in St. George Parish

Granted on September 6, 1774   Grant Book M, page 374

200 acres bounded on the north by ---- Sapp and south by
Samuel Lockhart.

****

Taylor, John
150 acres in St. George Parish

Surveyed on September 15, 1769   Plat Book C, page 372
Granted on August 2, 1774   Grant Book M, page 262

150 acres bounded on all sides by vacant land.

****

Telfair, Edward, Basil Cowper and William Telfair
150 acres in St. George Parish

Granted on March 4, 1771   Grant Book I, page 265

150 acres bounded on all sides by vacant land.

****

Telfair, William
200 acres in St. George Parish

Surveyed on March 28, 1765   Plat Book C, page 100
Granted on December 1, 1767   Grant Book F, page 428

200 acres bounded on the south by Briar Creek, west by land heretofore ordered to John Conyers and on every other side by vacant land at the time of the survey being heretofore ordered Aaron Jackson.

****

Telfair, William, Basil Cowper and Edward Telfair
150 acres in St. George Parish

Granted on March 4, 1771   Grant Book I, page 265

150 acres bounded on all sides by vacant land.

****

Thomas, Daniel
100 acres in St. George Parish

Granted on March 5, 1771   Grant Book I, page 276

100 acres bounded on all sides by vacant land.

****

Thomas, Daniel
200 acres in St. George Parish

Surveyed on July 12, 1773   Plat Book C, page 278
Granted on July 5, 1774   Grant Book M, page 128

200 acres bounded on the southwest by the Ogechee River and on the northwest by Sir James Wright.

****

Thomas, David
150 acres in St. George Parish

Surveyed on November 29, 1759   Plat Book C, page 427

150 acres bounded on the northeast by Savannah River. Original warrant states that tract is located on the Savannah River opposite Mathews Bluff on the Carolina side about three miles below land granted John Branson.

****

Thomas, Gideon
200 acres in St. George Parish

Surveyed on August 29, 1768   Plat Book C, page 365

200 acres bounded on the northwest by Nathaniel Hooker and
the corner of John Hooker's line.

****

Thomas, Gilshot
200 acres in St. George Parish

Granted on October 2, 1764   Grant Book E, page 53

200 acres bounded on the west by Briar Creek and east by
James McHenry.

****

Thomas, Gilshot
150 acres in St. George Parish

Surveyed on April 14, 1772   Plat Book C, page 355
Granted on September 6, 1774   Grant Book M, page 373

150 acres bounded on the southwest by Gilshot Thomas, southeast by ---- McHenry, and northeast by ---- David.

****

Thomas, Guilshot
150 acres in St. George Parish

Surveyed on September 17, 1767   Plat Book C, page 368
Granted on January 7, 1772   Grant Book I, page 505

150 acres bounded on the west by Briar Creek, northwest by
Guilshot Thomas and land of Asbile and northeast by Andrew
McCurrie and Miller.

****

Thomas, Joanna
200 acres - no location given, but probably St. George

Surveyed on August 10, 1759   Plat Book C, page 441

200 acres bounded on the northeast by David Emanuel. Original warrant states that the tract is located on a branch of Brier Creek, the south side.

****

Thomas, John
50 acres in St. George Parish

Granted on November 2, 1762   Grant Book D, page 239

50 acres bounded on the northwest by Joshua Atkinson and south-west by Hugh Ross.

****

Thomas, John
200 acres in St. George Parish

Granted on August 5, 1766   Grant Book E, page 346

200 acres bounded on all sides by vacant land.

****

Thomas, John
150 acres in St. George Parish

Granted on August 5, 1766   Grant Book E, page 347

150 acres bounded on the southwest by John Atkinson and northeast by William Addams.

****

Thomas, John
300 acres in St. George Parish

Surveyed on September 9, 1765   Plat Book C, page 365
Granted on November 4, 1766   Grant Book E, page 404

300 acres bounded on the north by John Thomas, Jr. Plat states that this was surveyed for John Thomas, Sr.

****

Thomas, John, Jr.
200 acres in St. George Parish

Surveyed on October 11, 1768 Plat Book C, page 368
Granted on May 2, 1769   Grant Book G, page 322

200 acres bounded on the north and west by William Rains, south by Hugh Ross and east by Joseph Atkinson.

****

Thomason, Laban
100 acres in St. George Parish

Surveyed on March 19, 1773 Plat Book C, page 378

100 acres bounded on one side by Beaverdam Creek, on one side by a branch and on one side by Flat Branch.

****

Thompson, George and Joseph Thompson
300 acres in St. George Parish

Granted on November 1, 1774 Grant Book M, page 745

300 acres bounded on the southwest by William Hobbs.

****

Thompson, James
100 acres in St. George Parish

Surveyed on June 14, 1769 Plat Book C, page 369
Granted on July 3, 1770   Grant Book I, page 112

100 acres in the Township of Queensborough bounded on the east by Reedy Branch, south by Thomas Beatty and north by John Bartholomew, and also Town Lot 51 in Queensborough.

****

Thompson, John
150 acres in St. George Parish

Surveyed on June 10, 1773 Plat Book C, page 378

150 acres bounded on one side by Allen Grove.

****

Thompson, Joseph and George Thompson
300 acres in St. George Parish

Granted on November 1, 1774   Grant Book M, page 745

300 acres bounded on the southwest by William Hobbs.

****

Thompson, Nicodemus
200 acres in St. George Parish

Surveyed on August 4, 1769   Plat Book C, page 367
Granted on October 3, 1769   Grant Book G, page 445

200 acres bounded on the southwest by James Oglebe and vacant
land and on the southeast by ---- Mercer.

****

Thomson, Solomon
300 acres in St. George Parish

Surveyed on May 28, 1770   Plat Book C, page 370
Granted on October 6, 1772   Grant Book I, page 756

300 acres bounded on the northeast by James Bennett and southeast by Thomas Colson.

****

Thorn, David
200 acres in St. George Parish

Granted on August 6, 1771   Grant Book I, page 394

200 acres bounded on the southwest by the Ogechee River.

****

Tilly, Joseph
150 acres in St. George Parish

Surveyed on March 8, 1771   Plat Book C, page 376
Granted on January 3, 1775   Grant Book M, page 949

150 acres bounded on all sides by vacant land.

****

Todd, John
100 acres in St. George Parish

Granted on September 6, 1774   Grant Book M, page 376

100 acres in the Township of Queensborough bounded on the
northeast by ---- Sharp and unknown land, northwest by ----
Bailey and southeast by ---- Sharp and vacant land.

****

Todd, William
100 acres in St. George Parish

Surveyed on January 9, 1769   Plat Book C, page 367
Granted on May 2, 1769   Grant Book G, page 321

100 acres bounded on the northwest by John Mackay.

****

Tomlinson, Samuel
150 acres in St. George Parish

Granted on May 7, 1765   Grant Book E, page 148

150 acres bounded on all sides by vacant land.

****

Tomlinson, Samuel
150 acres in St. George Parish

Granted on July 4, 1769   Grant Book G, page 373

150 acres bounded on the east by the said Samuel Tomlinson.

****

Tomlinson, Samuel
150 acres in St. George Parish

Surveyed on May 15, 1770   Plat Book C, page 373
Granted on August 2, 1774   Grant E   page 264

150 acres bounded on the south by ---- Pooler, north by the said Samuel Tomlinson and ---- Parkinson and south by the Savannah River. The same heretofore surveyed for the said Smauel Tomlinson and afterwards ordered to John Newman. The plat shows that the tract was bounded on the south by the Great Ogechee River and not the Savannah River.

****

Tomlinson, Samuel
150 acres in St. George Parish

Surveyed on March 30, 1769   Plat Book C, page 368

150 acres bounded on the north by Mr. Parkinson and on the south by the said Samuel Tomlinson.

****

Torquintz, Peter
100 acres in St. George Parish

Granted on December 6, 1757   Grant Book A, page 502

100 acres in the District of Halifax and bounded on the east by the Savannah River.

****

Tubeau, Ann
400 acres in St. George Parish

Surveyed on June 19, 1770   Plat Book M, page 49
Granted on November 1, 1774   Grant Book M, page 746

400 acres granted in trust to John Tubeau, for Samuel, Charles and Ann Tubeau.

****

Tubeau, Charles
400 acres in St. George Parish

Surveyed on June 19, 1770   Plat Book M, page 49
Granted on November 1, 1774   Grant Book M, page 746

400 acres granted to John Tubeau in trust for Samuel, Charles and Ann Tubeau.

Tubeau, John
400 acres in St. George Parish

Surveyed on June 19, 1770   Plat Book M, page 49
Granted on November 1, 1774   Grant Book M, page 746

400 acres granted to John Tubeau in trust for Samuel, Charles
and Ann Tubeau.

****

Tubeau, Samuel
400 acres in St. George Parish

Surveyed on June 19, 1770   Plat Book M, page 49
Granted on November 1, 1774   Grant Book M, page 746

400 acres granted in trust to John Tubeau for Samuel, Charles
and Ann Tubeau.

****

Turner, Venerias
100 acres in St. George Parish

Granted on September 6, 1774   Grant Book M, page 379

100 acres bounded on the northwest by George Wyche and on the
south by ---- Jones.

****

Tweedy, Esther
350 acres in St. George Parish

Surveyed on October 27, 1772   Plat Book C, page 354
Granted on September 6, 1774   Grant Book M, page 375

350 acres bounded on the northeast by ---- Hollingsworth.

****

Underwood, Daniel
150 acres in St. George Parish

Granted on October 29, 1765   Grant Book E, page 305

150 acres bounded on all sides by vacant land.

Underwood, Sarah
150 acres in St. George Parish

Granted on December 3, 1771   Grant Book I, page 485

150 acres bounded on the southeast by William Underwood.

****

Underwood, Sarah
100 acres in St. George Parish

Surveyed on June 2, 1773   Plat Book M, page 37
Granted on September 6, 1774   Grant Book M, page 381

100 acres bounded on the northwest by George Walker.

****

Underwood, William
100 acres in St. George Parish

Granted on June 5, 1770   Grant Book I, page 38

100 acres bounded on all sides by vacant land.

****

Upton, George
200 acres in St. George Parish

Surveyed on October 5, 1764   Plat Book M, page 65
Granted on June 5, 1765   Grant Book E, page 168

200 acres bounded on the south by the Great Ogechee River and east by Robert Heaton.

****

Von Munch Margaretha Barbara
647½ acres in St. George Parish

Granted on August 3, 1762   Grant Book D, page 159

647½ acres near a place called the Indian Small Corn House, known by the name of Peters Hoff, bounded on the south by James McHenry and on the east by a lagoon running into the Savannah River.

****

Wade, Nehemiah
250 acres in St. George Parish

Granted on September 6, 1774   Grant Book M, page 390

250 acres bounded on all sides by vacant land.

****

Walker, George
100 acres in St. George Parish

Surveyed on May 23, 1758   Plat Book C, page 429
Granted on February 5, 1760   Grant Book E, page 384

100 acres bounded on the northeast by Bryar Creek.

****

Walker, George
200 acres in St. George Parish

Surveyed on December 17, 1766   Plat Book M, page 50
Granted on April 7, 1767   Grant Book F, page 213

200 acres bounded on all sides by vacant land.

****

Walker, George
100 acres in St. George Parish

Granted on December 6, 1768   Grant Book G, page 241

100 acres bounded on the north by the said George Walker.

****

Walker, George
100 acres in St. George Parish

Granted on December 6, 1768   Grant Book G, page 242

100 acres bounded on the northeast by Daniel Underwood.

****

Walker, Joel
300 acres in St. George Parish

Granted on August 1, 1769   Grant Book G, page 401

300 acres bounded on the west by Robert House.

****

Walker, Joel
100 acres in St. George Parish

Granted on May 4, 1773   Grant Book I, page 999

100 acres bounded on the east by Charles Walker, north by
James Castilow and west by the said grantee.

****

Walker, Joseph
750 acres in St. George Parish

Granted on March 6, 1770   Grant Book G, page 569

750 acres bounded on the northeast by John Rae and Hugh
Ross, northwest and northeast by William Burney and southeast by Thomas Irwin.

****

Wall, Arthur
350 acres in St. George Parish

Granted on May 3, 1768   Grant Book G, page 111

350 acres bounded on the north by Briar Creek.

****

Wall, William
200 acres in St. George Parish

Granted on August 2, 1774   Grant Book M, page 265

200 acres bounded on all sides by vacant land.

****

Wall, William
100 acres in St. George Parish

Granted on October 4, 1774   Grant Book M, page 609

100 acres bounded on the north by Colson.

****

Wallicon, Daniel
100 acres in St. George Parish

Granted on July 2, 1765   Grant Book E, page 191

100 acres bounded on the northeast by the Savannah River and
on the northwest by Alexander LaMarr.

****

Walters, John
150 acres in St. George Parish

Granted on May 1, 1764   Grant Book E, page 9

150 acres bounded on the north by the Savannah River.

****

Warnell, Joseph
100 acres in St. George Parish

Granted on April 5, 1768   Grant Book G, page 88

100 acres bounded on all sides by vacant land.

****

Warnock, John
200 acres in St. George Parish

Granted on September 2, 1766   Grant Book E, page 375

200 acres bounded on the east by Jacob Kettle and on the
north by John Moore.

****

Warnock, Robert
150 acres in St. George Parish

Granted on July 3, 1770   Grant Book I, page 113

150 acres in the Township of Queensborough bounded on the east by Lambeths Creek and also Town Lot 50 in the Town of Queensborough.

****

Warren, Benjamin
100 acres in St. George Parish

Granted on December 6, 1774   Grant Book M, page 835

100 acres bounded on the north by Brier Creek.

****

Warren, Benjamin
150 acres in St. George Parish

Granted on January 3, 1775   Grant Book M, page 968

150 acres bounded on all sides by vacant land.

****

Waters, James
100 acres in St. George Parish

Granted on May 5, 1772   Grant Book I, page 611

100 acres bounded on the southeast by Joseph Bailey.

****

Waters, John
150 acres in St. George Parish

Granted on May 3, 1768   Grant Book G, page 113

150 acres bounded on the east by James Roberts.

****

Watson, Charles
650 acres in St. George Parish

Granted on July 4, 1769   Grant Book G, page 377

650 acres bounded on the south by the said Charles Watson.

****

Watson, Charles
150 acres in St. George Parish

Granted on July 4, 1769   Grant Book G, page 378

150 acres bounded on the northwest by land ordered the said Charles Watson and southwest by the Ogechee River.

****

Weathers, Edward
50 acres in St. George Parish

Granted on August 2, 1774   Grant Book H, page 112

50 acres bounded on all sides by vacant land.

****

Weathers, Edward
200 acres in St. George Parish

Granted on June 5, 1770   Grant Book I, page 37

200 acres bounded on all sides by vacant land.

****

Webb, William
200 acres in St. George Parish

Granted on July 7, 1767   Grant Book F, page 307

200 acres bounded on the east by the Savannah River, north by land laid out for a Glebe and south by William McDonald.

*****

Wells, Absalom
200 acres in St. George Parish

Granted on May 5, 1767   Grant Book F, page 262

200 acres bounded on all sides by vacant land.

****

Wells, George
100 acres in St. George Parish

Granted on May 4, 1773   Grant Book I, page 1001

100 acres bounded on all sides by vacant land.

****

Wells, John
200 acres in St. George Parish

Granted on October 29, 1765   Grant Book E, page 306

200 acres bounded on the north by Bryar Creek.

****

Wells, John
100 acres in St. George Parish

Granted on April 5, 1768   Grant Book G, page 90

100 acres bounded on all sides by vacant land.

****

Wells, Mary
100 acres in St. George Parish

Granted on January 3, 1775   Grant Book M, page 969

100 acres bounded on the west by the widow Thompson.

****

Wells, Mary
100 acres in St. George Parish

Granted on September 6, 1774   Grant Book M, page 392

100 acres bounded on all sides by vacant land.

                         ****

Wertsch, John
85 acres in St. George Parish

Granted on August 7, 1770   Grant Book H, page 47

85 acres bounded on the northeast by the Savannah River,
west by John Bradley and south by Robert ----.

                         ****

Whitehead, Reason
200 acres in St. George Parish

Granted on September 1, 1767   Grant Book F, page 370

200 acres bounded on all sides by vacant land.

                         ****

Whitehead, Reason
100 acres in St. George Parish

Granted on July 5, 1774   Grant Book M, page 139

100 acres bounded on all sides by vacant land.

                         ****

Whitehead, Thomas
200 acres in St. George Parish

Granted on May 7, 1765   Grant Book E, page 143

200 acres bounded on all sides by vacant land.

                         ****

Wiggins, Jesse
200 acres in St. George Parish

Granted on October 29, 1765   Grant Book E, page 309

200 acres bounded on all sides by vacant land.

                              ****

Williams, Asa
150 acres in St. George Parish

Granted on August 2, 1774   Grant Book M, page 273

150 acres bounded on the north by ---- Roberts and east by
the said Asa Williams.

                              ****

Williams, Charles
100 acres in St. George Parish

Granted on July 5, 1774   Grant Book M, page 135

100 acres bounded on the southwest by Catherine Johnson.

                              ****

Williams, George
250 acres in St. George Parish

Granted on January 2, 1770   Grant Book G, page 511

250 acres bounded on the northwest by David Howell and on
the south by John Tanner.

                              ****

Williams, John
300 acres in St. George Parish

Granted on August 7, 1764   Grant Book E, page 26

300 acres bounded on the north by Savannah River, east by
James Nesmith and south by Henry Sumerly.

                              ****

Williams, John
231 acres in St. George Parish

Granted on September 3, 1765   Grant Book E, page 243

231 acres bounded on the northeast by the Savannah River,
west by John Royal and east by John Mainer.

****

Williams, John
100 acres in St. George Parish

Granted on October 29, 1765   Grant Book E, page 387

100 acres bounded on the east by the Savannah River, west
by John Mainor and south by the said John William s.

****

Williams, John
100 acres in St. George Parish

Granted on November 1, 1774   Grant Book M, page 758

100 acres bounded on the northwest by Bryar Creek and east
by Francis Parish.

****

Williams, William
300 acres in St. George Parish

Granted on July 7, 1767   Grant Book F, page 308

300 acres bounded on the western corner by Bryar Creek.

****

Williams, William
800 acres in St. George Parish

Granted on March 7, 1769   Grant Book G, page 293

800 acres bounded on the northeast by the said William
Williams.

****

Williamson, Benjamin
250 acres in St. George Parish

Granted on February 5, 1760   Grant Book B, page 379

250 acres bounded on the northeast by Savannah River, southeast by Thomas Red and northwest by William Newberry.

****

Williamson, Benjamin
100 acres in St. George Parish

Surveyed on February 16, 1761   Plat Book C, page 429
Granted on August 7, 1764   Grant Book E, page 19

100 acres bounded on the southwest by Andrew Griener, west
by Savannah River, northwest by Richard Hubbart and north,
northeast, south and southeast by Kings Creek.

****

Williamson, Benjamin
100 acres in St. George Parish

Granted on November 3, 1767   Grant Book F, page 415

100 acres bounded on the west by land the said Benjamin
Williamson hath purchased of Robert Bevill and northeast
by Peter Blyth.

****

Williamson, Benjamin
200 acres in St. George Parish

Granted on August 2, 1774   Grant Book M, page 272

200 acres bounded on the northeast by the said Benjamin
Williamson and land surveyed for Nathaniel Miller.

****

Willson, Seth
100 acres in St. George Parish

Granted on September 6, 1774   Grant Book M, page 391

****

228

Wilson, John
350 acres in St. George Parish

Granted on August 2, 1774   Grant Book M, page 274

350 acres in the Township of Queensborough bounded on the
northeast by John McClelacon, northwest by Crossley and
southwest by John Maneely.

****

Wilson, Margaret
300 acres in St. George Parish

Granted on November 1, 1774   GRant Book M, page 756

300 acres bounded on the northwest by Edward Weathers.

****

Wimberly, Isaac
100 acres in St. George Parish

Granted on August 4, 1767   Grant Book F, page 335

100 acres bounded on all sides by vacant land.

****

Wimberly, Isaac
150 acres in St. George Parish

Granted on August 1, 1769   Grant Book G, page 402

150 acres bounded on the southwest by Jethro Roundtree
and Thomas Wimberly.

****

Wimberly, Isaac
300 acres in St. George Parish

Granted on October 4, 1774   Grant Book M, page 611

300 acres bounded on the west by William Penill and south
by Isaac Wimberly.

****

Wimberly, Thomas
150 acres in St. George Parish

Granted on June 2, 1767   Grant Book F, page 284

150 acres bounded on the northwest by Roundtree.

****

Winfree, Jacob
375 acres in St. George Parish

375 acres on Lamborts Creek bounded at the time of the
survey on every side by land vacant which said tract was
heretofore ordered Joseph Burton.

****

Winn, John Jr.
200 acres in St. George Parish

Granted on May 5, 1772   Grant Book I, page 610

200 acres bounded on all sides by vacant land.

****

Wolfington, Thomas
350 acres in St. George Parish

Granted on May 4, 1773   Grant Book I, page 1000

350 acres bounded on the northeast by Whitehead and John
Gretion.

****

Womack, Jesse
100 acres in St. George Parish

Surveyed on January 5, 1770   Plat Book M, page 9
Granted on June 5, 1770   Grant Book I, page 39

100 acres bounded on the northwest by Richard Womack, southwest by John Roberts and southeast by John Emanuel.

****

Womack, John
100 acres in St. George Parish

Granted on September 3, 1771   Grant Book I, page 419

100 acres bounded on the northwest by John Emanuel and
southwest by Richard Womack and Peter Grant.

****

Womack, Richard
300 acres in St. George Parish

Surveyed on February 13, 1769   Plat Book M, page 20
Granted on April 4, 1769   Grant Book G, page 308

300 acres bounded on all sides by vacant land.

****

Womack, Richard
150 acres in St. George Parish

Granted on May 2, 1769   Grant Book G, page 323

150 acres bounded on the east by Peter Grant and west by
John Emanuel.

****

Womack, Richard
250 acres in St. George Parish

Surveyed on August 17, 1769   Plat Book M, page 20
Granted on September 1, 1772   Grant Book I, page 743

250 acres bounded on the southeast and partly on the northeast by the said Richard Womack and northwest by Jared Irvin.

****

Wood, Alexander
100 acres in St. George Parish

Granted on April 3, 1764   Grant Book D, page 407

100 acres bounded on the northeast by the Savannah River.

****

Wood, David
300 acres in St. George Parish

Granted on May 7, 1771   Grant Book I, page 334

300 acres in the Township of Queensborough bounded on the northwest by the corner of the land of James Finley.

****

Wood, Isaac
100 acres in St. Paul and St. George Parishes

Granted on November 1, 1768   Grant Book G, page 222

100 acres bounded on all sides by vacant land.

****

Wood, Isaac
100 acres in St. George Parish

Granted on September 6, 1774   Grant Book M, page 385

100 acres in the Township of Queensborough bounded on the northwest by David Wood.

****

Woods, Thomas
250 acres in St. George Parish

Granted on August 2, 1774   Grant Book M, page 275

250 acres bounded on the northeast by Isaac Perry.

****

Wyche, George
200 acres in St. George Parish

Granted on February 2, 1768   Grant Book G, page 31

200 acres bounded on the southwest by Francis Wynne.

****

Wyche, George
200 acres in St. George Parish

Granted on April 2, 1771   Grant Book I, page 295

200 acres bounded on the north by Dunlap.

****

Wylly, Alexander
1500 partly in St. Matthew and partly in St. George Parishes

Granted on July 7, 1767   Grant Book F, page 306

1500 acres bounded on the east by Lewis Johnson, west partly
by land of Catherine Mullryne and on every other side by
vacant land.

****

Wylly, William
300 acres in St. George Parish

Granted on August 2, 1774   Grant Book M, page 271

300 acres bounded on the southeast by ---- Howell and southwest by Captain Horton.

****

Wynne, Francis
300 acres in St. George Parish

Granted on September 2, 1766   Grant Book E, page 374

300 acres bounded on the southeast by Beaverdam Branch and
Daniel Lott.

****

Wynne, Francis
200 acres in St. George Parish

Granted on May 5, 1767   Grant Book F, page 260

200 acres bounded on the southeast by Francis Jenkins.

****

Wynne, Francis
100 acres in St. George Parish

Granted on June 7, 1768   Grant Book G, page 130

100 acres bounded on all sides by vacant land.

****

Wynne, Peter
300 acres in St. George Parish

Granted on October 29, 1765   Grant Book E, page 274

300 acres bounded on all sides by vacant land.

****

Wynne, Peter
250 acres in St. George Parish

Granted on May 5, 1767   Grant Book F, page 258

250 acres on Rocky Creek bounded on every side by land
vacant at the time of the survey which said tract was
heretofore ordered Priscilla Jones, Spinster.

****

Wynne, Peter
200 acres in St. George Parish

Granted on February 2m 1768   Grant Book G, page 32

200 acres bounded on all sides by vacant land.

****

Wynne, Peter, Jr.
200 acres in St. George Parish

Granted on May 5, 1767   Grant Book F, page 261

200 acres bounded on the southeast and northeast by Aaron
Penson and southwest by Peter Wynne, Sr.

****

Yarborough, Manoah
100 acres in St. George Parish

Granted on June 5, 1771   Grant Book I, page 354

100 acres bounded on the southwest by the Ogechee River.

****

Yonge, Henry, Jr.
200 acres in St. George Parish

Granted on October 3, 1769   Grant Book G, page 450

200 acres bounded on the northeast by Paul Haroldson.

****

Yonge, Henry, Sr.
500 acres in St. George Parish

Granted on April 2, 1771   Grant Book I, page 297

500 acres bounded on the east by lands partly of Nicholas
Cavenah and on all other sides by land vacant.

****

Young, James
150 acres in St. George Parish

Granted on October 3, 1769   Grant Book G, page 452

150 acres bounded on the southeast by John Nelson and southwest by John Duhart.

****

Young, John
250 acres in St. George Parish

Granted on September 1, 1767   Grant Book F, page 372

250 acres bounded on the southeast partly by John Penny
and on every other side by land vacant.

****

Young, Peter
300 acres in St. George Parish

Granted on September 5, 1769   Grant Book G, page 420

300 acres bounded on the northwest by Arthur Wall and on the southeast by John Rae.

****

Young, William
300 acres in St. George Parish

Granted on October 3, 1769   Grant Book G, page 451

300 acres bounded on the east by Solomon Prethro.

****

Young, William
150 acres in St. George Parish

Granted on April 7, 1772   Grant Book I, page 577

150 acres bounded in part on the northeast by David Lewis and on all other sides by land vacant.

******
****

www.ingramcontent.com/pod-product-compliance
Lightning Source LLC
Chambersburg PA
CBHW080417270326
41929CB00018B/3065